THE
ROAD
WE TRAVELED

THE
ROAD
WE TRAVELED

A Memoir of Two Worlds

By
Uchendu Precious Onuoha

iUniverse, Inc.
Bloomington

The Road We Traveled
A Memoir of Two Worlds

iUniverse books may be ordered through booksellers or by contacting:

iUniverse
1663 Liberty Drive
Bloomington, IN 47403
www.iuniverse.com
1-800-Authors (1-800-288-4677)

Because of the dynamic nature of the Internet, any web addresses or links
contained in this book may have changed since publication and may no longer be
valid. The views expressed in this work are solely those of the author and do not
necessarily reflect the views of the publisher, and the publisher hereby disclaims any
responsibility for them.

Any people depicted in stock imagery provided by Thinkstock are models, and such
images are being used for illustrative purposes only.
Certain stock imagery © Thinkstock.

ISBN: 978-1-4759-7835-3 (sc)
ISBN: 978-1-4759-7836-0 (ebk)

Library of Congress Control Number: 2013903362

Printed in the United States of America

iUniverse rev. date: 05/07/2013

CONTENTS

DEDICATION

This work is dedicated to my precious wife, Anthonia Nkiru and my wonderful daughter Annabel Ucheoma Uchendu in appreciation of their undying love, encouragement, patience and support-especially the times when my work and assignments ran deep into the night, and denied them the warmth and comfort of my presence at home.

To my dear parents, the late Elder Abraham Onuoha Nwosu and Agnes Onuoha, I thank you for your devotion to the Lord Jesus Christ.

To her Excellency, Bianca Odinaka Ojukwu, the first Nigeria female to become an ambassador to Spain, you have set the wheels in motion for the other Nigerian females who aspire to follow in your footsteps.

And to my elder sister Sarah Chi Ajiere, your virtues have been serendipitous in my life and you are a remarkable role model for young women everywhere.

Also to the rest of my brothers and sisters and in-laws who have always stood by me through thick and thin, I love you and appreciate the thickness of the blood that flows between us.

To my friend Anita Thompson for the transparent and true friendship we have shared as well as for your efforts in editing my work.

To the men and women of God who provided spiritual guidance and counsel, thank you for touching my life.

My thanks also to Dr.Karl Albertz and family for all the help you gave me during my stay in Germany.

Also my thanks to the Atlantic International University (AIU) staff who facilitated the acquisition of my Bachelor's degree. You know who you are! And thanks to a notable alumnus of AIU, her Excellency Joyce Banda, president of Malawi who is a precious woman and who has provided great motivation for me and many others.

And finally to all the outstanding journalists and media specialists (especially in Nigeria), you are my inspiration, and the light of the world, so keep the light shining!

PREFACE

To put together the ideas and materials for a book is a daunting task. It is conceived as an individual effort but in reality it is hatched for the public. Once the manuscript is handed over to the publisher, it becomes a business of opinion.

My motivation to write has come from the confidence developed in writing letters for parents to their siblings in the city, and girlfriends on behalf of some of my classmates in college. Also, as a child I was called (Ode akwukwo) meaning—"book writer" which is a form of humorous teasing for a child learning his first letters of the alphabet. My thanks go to the native women and parents who gave me an early start in writing for others.

"The dream in your heart may be bigger than the environment in which you find yourself in". Joel Osteen, (Pastor Lakewood Church, Texas U.S.A). www.twitter. com. The Road We Traveled is about a typical childhood in an African village and it is a compilation of events which spans 35 years in Nigeria and crescendos to my life abroad away from everything that was familiar.

I have written about my life experiences—past, present and future—to serve as a missing link to children born in a diaspora who may not have experienced the same birth circumstances as their parents. It will also be an eye-opener to others interested in knowing what childhood was like in Africa and how we all have challenges on our personal pilgrimages through life regardless of our continent or race. It is common to all of humanity.

"Those who are blessed with the soaring swiftness of an eagle and have flown before let them fly, I will journey slowly and I too will arrive". (Author Unknown)

The world is a veritable playground for us to fulfill the role assigned to us by divine providence. We may not all have the same smooth and level ground or rocky terraces allocated to us to accomplish our life roles within the time and space we occupy, but whatever be our lot we must till our ground to make it yield.

My purpose is to leave a footprint of honor and integrity for my daughter Annabel, and her siblings, descendants and others who may not have been born under the same circumstances nor had a difficult childhood. And my personal philosophy and mission statement is as Albert Einstein wrote, "stay the course, light a star, change the world wherever you are".

As it has been said, "No man is an island" and I would be remiss if I failed to acknowledge all the people who have in one way or another given me a helping hand and motivation, and have held the ladder for me to climb. Without your support and goodwill, I may not have come to this length.

I wish to thank Almighty who is the source of wisdom and knowledge in which I thrust, for giving me life, good health, spiritual, material, and intellectual resources to pursue my goals. To Him I owe all. To the elders and youths of Umuogele, the land of my birth, my hat is off to you!

PART 1

Family: Retrospective Experiences in Nigeria

BORN UNDER THE SHADOW
OF DEATH

" No matter how far a stream flows it never forgets its source", Eyamide Ella Lewis-Coker, African Proverbs, Parables and Wise Sayings (2011, Paperback). I was born about forty five years ago in Umuogele village of Igbo descent in the eastern region of Nigeria during the onset of Nigeria's emergence as an independent nation in 1960. It was around that time the Nigerian bloodbath started when the country plunged into a devastating genocide and civil war, a war that left no Igbo family without loss.

The Nigeria-Biafra war was a time when men's hearts failed them, especially the Igbo, as they were hunted, butchered, maimed, slaughtered like sheep in all parts of Nigeria. Many of their pregnant women were pierced with daggers and machetes while having their fetuses disemboweled. It was a time of genocide never known to any tribe in the history of Africa before. It was under such a gruesome circumstance that I came into the world. My delivery was at the home of Mgborogwu, an old woman who served as a tribal midwife as there were no clinics and hospitals for women in labor needing to deliver a child.

Because of this, children born at home did not have the luxury of sporting a birth certificate as there was not a birth record to mark the arrival of a child. Parents would mark a child's birth with the occurrence of a significant event. The difficult way of life while growing up in my native village leaves much to the imagination for one who has grown up with all the amenities of comfort! Imagine growing up without the basic amenities such as clean and abundant water, indoor plumbing, electricity, hospital services or educational opportunities. The village did not have a school, or a communal well; in fact we grew up with almost NO amenities.

Our source of water was the rain water that fell and the ponds in the area. Each family dug a big hole that would hopefully retain water for domestic use after each rainfall. The pond would retain this deluge of ground water for a few days and then dry up later. Otherwise, our water supply involved trekking long distances carrying clay and calabash pots to streams located far away in other communities to fetch water as my village had no stream. For our lighting needs, we had the sun by day and the moon and twinkling stars that lit the firmament by night.

While nature's torch lit our way in the sky at night, darkness within the home was reasonably kept at bay by cooking fires that roared and with oil lamps lit with the palm kernel oil we produced. Native herbalists were our health care practitioners and were well-versed in the knowledge of which herb and root would cure sickness. For shelter, each family had a crude house with a thatched roof—a shelter that was less than ideal during the rainy season, as rain water used to seep through and drench us through and through. It certainly made staying asleep an impossible task as the rain would wake us as it was just like taking a shower, but unwillingly!

Though my village lacked government presence in provision of basic amenities, nature did not deny us its benevolence as the land was very fertile and productive for agriculture. Numerous crops of yam, cassava, maize, melon, vegetables and mushrooms were plentiful and Mother Nature blessed and planted within our soil rich varieties of mushrooms which would sprout up seasonally to supplement our food. As a child, I enjoyed going to the bush with my mates to search and pluck the mushrooms which our mothers used to prepare soup for us. We also picked up snails from the bush, set traps, and hunted for bush meats. My daughter and her siblings will never understand the fun we had as her knowledge of food provision is the grocery store nearby.

Being born under these circumstances affected my childhood, and I saw the world as a place of hostility, suffering, hardship, and a place where one must take his fate into his own hands, and must be ready to suffer affliction and want in order to be able to survive. Do not pity me for the hardships and for what I endured, but rather rejoice with me as what I encountered at birth and childhood formed and fashioned me to be a man who does not rely much on others. Rather, I always strive for a way to succeed as an independent person, working to improve the lot of my family, village, and community.

"The deepest craving of the human spirit is to find a sense of significance and relevance. And the search for relevance in life is the ultimate pursuit of man." Myles Munroe, president and founder of the <u>Bahamas Faith Ministries International</u> (BFMI)

From my beginning, I was brought forth in a village founded by Ogele, the place I call home, the place that beckons to me still . . .

TRIBUTE TO MY OGELE LAND

Out of you spring forth life
In you I first breadth of life
In you I first saw the ray of light
My first education was in you
Religion you gave to me
Good morals of life I found in you
Democracy I tasted in you
Ogelecracy you gave to me
Diligence and devotion to duty
You taught me
Obedience and loyalty
To that which is good and right?
You gave to me
You taught me to strive for virtue
And to uphold sincerity of purpose and spirit
To embrace goodness
And to reject evil
To bring glory, honor
And not shame to you
Now, I am across the shore
Though far away
But my spirit lives daily in you
The foundation you laid for me
I daily build on

The candle of light
You gave to me is still on
Lightening the way for me
The good seeds you sowed in me
Are growing and will not be stunted
I am proud of you
And to be gotten of you
Though in a distant land
Unknown to you I am
Yet I dream of you daily
My spirit longs to
Tread my feet on you
And to drink wine from
The bowels of your love

Beloved Ogele
Dear Ogele
Great Ogele
I call on you thrice
Your child greets you
Great Okamgba
Great Osuoke,
I bow before you
I beckon on you to still hold
The light for your child
Like a pilgrim
In search of success I am
In a foreign land
Searching for the diamond fleas

I will come back to you
When I have found
I will return better than I left
Great Ogele
My love for you remains strong
You are the Genesis of my life
In you will I drop the last breath
And my remains will lie in you
When my life has run its circle
And I will sleep in you.

A NOTEWORTHY ANCESTRAL LINEAGE

My nuclear family was comprised of 12 individuals: my two parents, seven sisters and two brothers in addition to myself. Those of us who survived include three sisters, two brothers and me. I am the fourth among the surviving siblings with two younger sisters after me, and our mother continues to enjoy life even at her advanced age.

My mother only had one sibling, "papa Mark" as we called him. My maternal grandparents were well to do in terms of traditional wealth, having inherited much farmland from their family ancestors and this was passed on to my mother and her sibling. In those days wealth was measured in acres of land, groves of palm trees, goats, sheep and the number of yam barns in your possession.

Father also had great ancestors as his grandfather Okamgba was reputed to be the best wrestler and a great warrior. Okamgba was a direct descendant of Ogele, the founder of my village Umuogele. Father was the eldest among five children comprised of two sisters as well as two brothers and him. My late uncle Ogu was the youngest among them. With a scintillating personality, he had been a teacher before the war, a good sportsman, and the one who kept the family in the know. Uncle Ogu, it is said, was a voice of inspiration.

As an infant, he was very fond of me and called me "Nwaoko" (man). Unfortunately, he died in the Biafra war which was a loss that affected the entire family's progress and future, as he would have helped father to sponsor our education. As a child, I always thought that uncle Ogu's long absence from home meant that he traveled. But in later years I came to realize that he indeed traveled to return no more as death is a journey of no return. We have lived a community life from the outset, and in the villages, it continues to this day.

THE BURDEN
OF EXTENDED FAMILY

Although the sense of family and community were innate and a strong force in my upbringing, it was not all idyllic or that of cupids, or hearts and flowers. Our sense of family and of belonging to each other was very strong but amidst the security, there were also very dysfunctional family members. One of my relatives had a very unhappy marriage, and you must remember that in this culture, especially at this time, marriage was forever. He was taciturn in words and peevish. Everything irritated him.

His home was like a war zone and a battle field as he and his wife often came to fists in a physical fight. To say that the wife was a nagging woman is not painting her strongly enough, as it does not give one the true picture. Her mouth went at the speed of a MIG missile whenever she spoke. Even when she was in a state of peace within herself, no one could withstand the velocity of her mouth under normal circumstances let alone when she was angry and riled. Their relationship was like an active volcano, with quarrels and fights erupting and spewing as hot lava between them both day and night. It wasn't uncommon for the neighbors to hear the clamoring of pots flying and being thrown against the wall, glass breaking and the cries for help emanating from their poor children during these marathon fight episodes.

The neighbors responded quickly and pulled the two battling foes apart. The disadvantage the husband had was that she was beyond his control in that not only could she hurl words of rage, but she was physically strong and agile as she was a hard-working woman and not given to a state of languor or laziness. Her farm was never overgrown with weeds as was the case of some lazy women. Despite her faults, she was diligent and jovial. As a child, I would think that if that's what marriage is like, is better for a man to remain single throughout his entire life. However," Only when you have crossed the river can you say the crocodile has a lump on his snout". African Proverbs in African Literature, www.proverbs africanliterature.wordpress.com

We lived a community life where families and kin lived together in one compound. The buildings faced each other and at the center was the family hut which the elders used for rest and receiving visitors. Living together meant that you were your brother's keeper, as your neighbors' problems affected you. Our buildings were the mud plastered thatched houses. There was a clear mark of distinction and identity between the owners of zinc houses and those who owned mud plastered thatched houses. Zinc houses were very few and were a mark of affluence.

And as mentioned earlier, there was no indoor plumbing for us. Our toilets were pit toilets located at the back of the yard. Fresh and dry leaves served as toilet tissue, as they were used as natural toilet paper to wipe one's buttocks. The leaves certainly were nothing like the toilet tissue sold in the

stores, but it served its purpose. We did not have electric
stoves or special ranges for indoor barbecuing. Smoke
would flood and billow throughout the house as the women
cooked with firewood, a cooking method for food which far
surpasses the fully equipped kitchen with all of the modern
appliances used today in my humble opinion.

The African's strong sense of family is a tie that binds you
literally to your family members and your extended family
in almost every aspect of life. It is like a fraternity second to
none. Problems were shared and inherited. Your brother's
problem was your problem equally. Sometimes this family
yoke that binds you together is the yoke that detains
you and halts your progress as you must think and live
collectively, but nonetheless it is an African trait and is one
of the major differences between the African black man
and some of the other cultures I eventually encountered.

I remember the story I was told about a hunter who caught
some white crabs and some black crabs and decided against
cooking them and let them go. He took them to the bank
of the river and covered them with two baskets respectively
and went home. The following morning as he came to the
river, he was shocked to observe that the white crabs had
all jumped into the river and escaped individually, while
the black crabs were holding each other struggling and
would pull their brother crab back in if they tried to escape.
Because of the burden to care for their brother crab, they
wasted precious time which could have been used to get
away and the hunter came and took them home for a feast.
That is how carrying extended family responsibilities
weigh down the African and pull him back from pursuing
his personal goals.

FARMING—THE IGBO
WAY OF LIFE

"He, who is not beaten by sun or rain, will eventually be beaten by hunger", Innocent Nkhonyo—The Wisdom of Africa, www.poemhunter.com. My parents were farmers as my father inherited much farmland from his ancestors. Though they were not affluent, we never lacked food to eat. They labored very hard to fend for us. They cultivated cassava, yam, cocoyam, melon vegetables and other food crops. In the beginning of the farming season, father would cut and clear the land with the help of my eldest brother. It would be allowed to dry for a time and then a fire was set to burn up the debris.

The burning of the old growth prepared the land to yield rich crops. Sometimes, the men used to take turns to help one another clear the brush at their respective farms during the farming season. On such occasions, the women would cook food and take it to them at the forest. When they came back in the evening, they settled down to a well prepared evening meal accompanied with the evening's fresh palm wine. We as children sat on the mat and listened to the stories of the past, about their ancestors, slave raids, and colonial incursion into Igbo land.

Farming was a collective effort. Many of the crops were considered women's work, but yam planting was considered the measure of man and his notoriety as a man's prowess in Igbo land was measured by the number of yam barns he had. Our farming method did not include tractors, or combines, but rather our crops were planted and harvested through the novel method of manual labor.

The large African family provided willing and unwilling farm hands to bring in the harvest. All hands had to be on deck. At times we were organized according to age and matched to a task fitting that age by our parents. My parents used to cultivate about ten to twelve parcels of land, which is between one to two acres in size. These parcels were located at different places and the lack of modern transportation made getting to and from the various farmlands a difficult task to accomplish and time was at a premium during growing season.

Our community had an abundance of palm trees and my father had palm trees growing on the family spreads. The harvesting and processing of oil from the palm fruits was an assiduous task, and not for the lazy or the sluggard. It was a communal exercise as the entire village usually set aside a day to harvest the palm fruit. Climbing the wild and tall palm trees with ropes was such a rigorous and risky job. Sometimes the ropes would break and the climber would fall and sustain serious injuries such as bone fractures, or even death. The day before the harvest, the professional palm harvesters were hired to survey the palm trees to locate the largest quantity of ripened palms.

The village woke up at the sound of the heart pounding "ekwe", (wooden gong). At the prompting of the "ekwe", the men and women and their hired palm harvesters came out at the village square where the village head admonished them not to trespass into neighboring community land to avoid the onset of trouble. Once the order was given to start, the harvesters rushed to the bush. It was like a war had been declared, with people shouting and hissing while cutting the palm fruits. The families gathered the palm bunches together as the men harvested. The skill and labor involved was very tasking and along with sustained possible injury from a fall, the harvesters also faced the dangers of snake bites.

The process had only begun with the harvesting of the fruits. After the fruits were taken home, another painstaking process of extracting the oil began. Father would cut the fruit one by one to separate the fruits from the strands in order to facilitate the hand picking of the fruit. You needed fine skills to extract the fruit, as the thorn-like tissues of the fruit could pierce the fingers which caused pain and injury of no other kind.

Several days were set aside to pound the palm fruit in a deep wooden trough with a huge pestle after boiling the fruits to soften them on a fire in a large metal pot. Our eyes were blood red from the smoke emitting in great blasts from the cooking fire as the pot needed to boil feverishly in order for the fruit to soften. I vividly remember father pounding the fruits so hard in the wooden trough with a thick, long wooden pestle that sweat ran down his body as though a water faucet had been turned on. He would pound away until the kernels covers peeled back and were mashed together.

Mother took time to separate the kernels during this process. She too would sweat profusely as she would squeeze the kernels strongly with her two hands to extract the oil. This manual extraction was a grueling process which required sweat and effort before the palm oil would come forth as a product used within the household. I never much cared for the suffering involved, but as is the case, they did what they had to do to survive.

After the Nigerian civil war, in addition to farming, father went into trading. He traded in stock fish, oil, yam, ropes and baskets. As a man gifted in craftsmanship, he made the ropes used for climbing and harvesting the tall palm trees which he sold to the palm harvesters. He combined these business ventures along with garri processing and marketing. **Garri** is a popular West-African food made from cassava tubers. The tubers are peeled, washed and grated or crushed to produce a mash. The mash is placed in a porous bag and allowed to ferment for one or two days and weighed down to press the water out.

The process continues with sifting, and roasting the garri. The resulting dry granular garri can be stored for long periods of time. Father was definitely an entrepreneur as he was well known in the entire village and community for his innovation, skill and prowess in processing cassava into garri. Father hired people who specialized in crushing the peeled cassava on hand-graters as the grating was a difficult and time consuming process and everything was processed manually. The arrival of the cassava grinding machine in the village did not occur until the late seventies and at that point, he increased his rate of garri production as he bought large quantities of cassava tubers from the local markets which were processed into garri and sold. Father was sought out as a well-known trader and frequent customers would visit our compound, looking for oil, stock fish, yam, garri, rope, and baskets.

THE PARENTS I KNOW

My father was always busy and had no time for frivolities as he had to work very hard to provide for his large family and ensure that we received post-secondary education. He was a man not given to wasting time as he always strived to be thorough and innovative in any task he undertook. His diligence and dedication to secular activities were his devotion and commitment to his Christianity. He was a devoted Christian who let the Word of God guide him as he embraced Christianity in his youth when the British missionaries came to the village. He never forgot to tell the story of a white missionary named "Whittler," which he pronounced as "Witilo".

Both my parents were devoted Christians who lived out their beliefs actively and we as their children were schooled in the Christian faith from infancy. Attending to early morning Saturday mission work was compulsory for us. And for no reason would we miss the Sunday church worship. I started the Monday and Tuesday baptismal classes quite early. I took part in the required three year preparatory Bible study class and exam before baptism and once I completed it, I was baptized. That helped me to be very good in religious knowledge. I recited bible chapters in the church during children's harvest and in school during morning devotions.

My father's devotion and adherence to the Christian faith was very strong and has always motivated me. It instilled in me the resolve to not follow the crowd, and to realize that public opinion wasn't necessarily correct. Just because a tradition or custom was popular and upheld by a people did not mean that the same tradition or custom was correct in principle, nor should it be followed simply because it was a tradition.

Abraham, as father was named, depicted the true qualities of his biblical predecessor, Abraham from the Bible. The biblical Abraham was known as a man of faith and a friend of God. Father lived up to the dictates of his name and faith. He left a legacy for me in particular to always stand firm in that which is right.

"Fading away like the stars of the morning, losing their light by the bright day sun, so shall we pass from the earth and its toiling, only remembered by what we have done". Horatius Bonar (1808-1889). The composer of that song may have had in mind the end of all men in mind. Father passed away on March 5, 2005 and though he is no more, he is constantly being remembered by his works and for his integrity.

He is well remembered in the village and its surroundings as Abraham the man who abolished the Mmaji custom and tradition in the community. Mmaji was a fetish custom practiced in some Igbo lands where females named "Mmaji" are depicted as outcasts and dedicated to idols. At death, any woman bearing this name was not supposed to be buried like a normal corpse but rather the head of Mmaji's body must not ever touch the ground as that would invoke a calamity on the land. According to traditional dictates, Mmaji's corpse would be taken to the forest and tied on a tree with a jar placed strategically under the head to catch it when it would fall.

Mmaji, my father's elder sister who had the misfortune of bearing that name, died in the sixties. At that time, the custom was very much in vogue and the villagers demanded that my father comply with the traditional burial rituals by hanging her body on a tree. He did not bend to the wishes of the villagers and sited that as a Christian he would not practice such a fetish custom. He insisted that his late sister was a human being and must receive a normal burial.

Father was firm and courageous in rejecting a practice that imposed a threat to his very existence. Being the principled type that he was, he told them that he must obey God rather than men. The villagers abandoned the corpse with a threat that if father failed to comply with the tribal custom within a week, something disastrous would happen to him as the gods would not stand for this break in tradition. To the surprise of everyone, a week passed and he buried his sister's corpse alone, but in normal burial fashion and with no imminent calamity.

The village waited in anticipation for the said expected calamity. Weeks ran into months and months into years and nothing happened to him. My father's example of standing true to his beliefs was used as a reference point to abolish the Mmaji tradition. Through that incident, I learnt from father that I must never allow myself to be intimidated by a popular or public opinion and never to follow the crowd blindly.

"Childhood is like a stream, if it's not directed to its course it meanders and swallows its tail" (African proverb). When I look back to the past, I remember some things I did that upset my parents and some things they liked about me. They always complained about my stubborn streak and strong will. I was a child who refused to do anything when asked, but rather only would do things when I felt like it. Incessant fights with my siblings and friends were the norm for me. My parents were thankful for some of my traits such as my lack of intimidation by children of my own age or older than me and that scholastically, I never trailed behind my comrades. I was adept at winning prizes in Sunday school bible quizzes and for always asked probing and intelligent questions. I also showed myself useful in domestic works, and hardly ever was graced by sickness.

These behaviors made father hard on me. Father firmly believed that if you spared the rod, you spoiled the child as stated in the Bible. And because he would not have me be a spoiled brat, I often felt the sting of his whip—especially at nights. I was agile and fleet of foot and father would have quite a time to catch me as I would run away when I knew that I had committed an offense. Pursuing me was like trying to catch a free range chicken.

Father was wise in his methods. He would often ignore my disobedience during the day and allowed me to feed very well and then go to bed in peace. I would think that he had forgotten and that this time I was safe . . . but then on the edge of falling asleep, he would grab me and would recall the day's occurrence and caned me. Of-course, I used to think that my father didn't love me due to the way he used to discipline me, but I later discovered otherwise.

"For whom the Lord loveth he chasteneth, and scourgeth every son whom he receiveth. Hebrews 12:6 <u>*King James Bible (Cambridge Ed.)*</u> Father really meant well for me and the rest of my siblings also, as he never displayed favoritism to any of us.

While father was strict and meticulous and he never socialized much. My mother exhibited an amazing sense of humor, as well as kindness and charity to a flaw. She is and always had been a lovely woman—caring, open hearted and ever ready to share whatever she had with others. Many native women and widows always came to ask her for food crops during the farming season and harvest and her generous heart made her give without measure.

Mother truly was father's help-meet as she worked and toiled by his side and took care of much of the farming chores, and was very active with women's group activities both in the village and church. She is talented in playing the ogene, an Igbo musical instrument which is a large metal bell, conical in shape and hollow inside. The iron body is usually struck with a soft wooden stick. She played for the native women dance groups during ceremonies honoring the newborns babies of the community.

Mother was also a business woman and during her younger years, she traded in crayfish and dry fish which she carried long distances to various markets to sell. On these occasions we always waited in anticipation for her return as she would buy cassava baked balls for us as a treat for doing our chores without having to be reminded to while she was away. The chores included cracking the palm kernels which mother sold or used to prepare palm jelly, a concoction we used as a sort of cream.

Along with the farm chores such as weeding and the gathering in of crops, we would bring firewood in from the forest and fetch water in calabash gourds and pots from faraway streams. Sometimes the fetching of water proved to be futile as the calabash gourd would fall off my head and break before we reached home.

Mother's door and heart was always open to people in need. The little she had, she shared with those who asked of her. However, she would not ask or borrow anything from others. Even in extreme cases of lack, she would prefer to manage with what she had. My parents taught us to be resourceful, self-reliant and to be content with what we have.

Mother was my first educator, teacher, and confidante as I felt so free to confide and share my heart feelings with her. Sweet mother, I will never forget the pains and sufferings you went through with father for me and the rest of your children. God bless the day Father found you. And for this cause, I urge children all over the world to appreciate the labor and sacrifice of parents in nurturing them from infancy to maturity and the global family should acknowledge the unique role of a woman as a mother is the only channel mankind comes into the world. To their credit I dedicate the composition below:

THE ROAD WE CAME

All men great and small
Colors, black and white
the strong and feeble
Beautiful and ugly
the wise and foolish
all the motley human family
came through your pathway
once crossed, never re-crossed.

A runway for life's plane
flying life into existence
An ocean way large
Sailing life's boat and ship across
The railers rail
Railing men into earth's station
a road life's vehicle and footmen
daily run and walk to mother earth
Once crossed, never re-crossed

Mother´s photo

King and kings
Prince and princess
With the soaring swiftness of an eagle
On flight earth bound
Flew across your green line
Noblemen, captains and men of great
On earth bound ship
Sailed through your pathway
Once crossed, never re-crossed.

Life's express-way
A journey on your path
lasts for nine moons
A bridge between life
Never ever-been and ever to be
The mother womb, a mother bridge
The mother road
The road I know
The road we came
Once crossed, never re-crossed.

CUSTOMS AND FESTIVALS

My village and community had some customs and festivals that were observed and celebrated which I witnessed during my childhood. Community life was not all work and no play, but rather it had moments of fun and recreation where people rejoiced and celebrated in the revelry. These occasions included the new yam festival, birth celebrations, after birth care, and marriage ceremonies to name a few. These customs and festivals used to be happy events and appealed to me as a child but now I miss them and I wish I could relive them once more. Moreover, some of these festivals are no longer observed as the church played down some of them.

THE NEW YAM FESTIVAL

T he yam is a staple of the Nigerian and West African diet. In Nigeria, in many yam-producing areas, it is said that "yam is food and food is yam." Wikipedia reference. Yam is not cheap to cultivate as a considerable portion of each harvest has to be kept for planting and reproduction the following year. Yam has always been a very precious crop and if for any reason its yield failed, the community was destined for starvation.

A rich yam harvest was a sign of prowess for a man. The community usually conferred such titles like "Diji" (yam husband) or "Eze ji" (yam king) as a mark of honor on outstanding yam farmers. The New Yam festival was one of the major festivals celebrated by the community. It was a sacred event used in thanking God for a successful farming season and harvest. It marked the end of the season of scarcity and the beginning of season of bounty. We looked forward to the day of this festival.

Elaborate preparations were made. Families invited their relatives, in-laws and friends. The men made arrangements to supply palm wine and kola nuts. The women weeded and swept the road paths and the village square. On the festival day, the villagers wore their best apparel. Some would kill their fowl or a goat to prepare assorted varieties of yam dishes such as pounded yam, roasted yam, yam porridge, African salad and pepper soup. And of course the palm wine flowed.

The sound of the Ikoro gong summoned people to gather at the village square. The festival used to be declared open by the traditional ruler and elders who poured out a libation of wine and offered kola nuts to their ancestors thanking them for granting the community a bountiful harvest. Usually the eldest kinsman would be asked to present and bless the kola-nut as follows:,

"Olisa di nelu (The God of host) we thank you for the new yam. He who brings kola

has brought a good thing. As it is good today may it be good tomorrow. Let the kite perch and let the eagle perch, but anyone that says that the other one should not perch, let its wing be broken. Live and let live, men, women, and folks shall be. The water shall be, and the fish shall be. Let the water not dry and let the fish not die. He who is cutting the "Ngwu" tree for no just cause, may his cutlass remain blunt.

Anybody planning or thinking evil, may the evil befall on him. May the road be straight for all of us. He who misjudged anybody may he be misjudged too. He who heard and pretended not to hear, may he have ear problems. He who saw and said he did not see, may he have eye problems. He who knew and claimed not to know, may he lose his mind. May the evil men not be at rest until they stop their evil practice. May the evil somebody does rest upon his head . . . In conclusion he beckoned on the ancestors to take the kola-nut."

Elders Cutting the Yam during a New Yam Festival

Cultural dances were performed to entertain the people. Everyone ate, drank, and visited relatives and friends and everybody would rejoice during this time. For children, it used to be such a happy event for us to eat meat and enjoy delicious foods. Also it provided opportunity for us to know our extended families. We celebrated the New Yam festival not because it would be impossible to eat our yams without the festival but because of the significance this ceremony had in our lives and culture.

BIRTH CELEBRATION

"The labor of childbirth is known to the mother". Jeanne Ukwendu, African Proverbs on Pregnancy and Birth, www.bellaonline.com. The birth of a newborn baby was welcomed by ceremony in my tribe. It was a great joy for a woman to deliver safely. The joy was more intense if a male child was born as the birth of a male child was seen as a continuation of the family's heritage or lineage. Couples without a male child did not feel happy until they would have a son to carry on the family name. It was believed that a girl would leave the family sooner or later to bear her husband's name but the boy is a permanent man of the family who would continue wherever the father stopped. On such occasion the husband would shoot his gun off once or twice to announce the birth while the mother in-law would start shouting in tandem with her hands tapping her cheeks;

Ooooh, ooooh, ooooh

Ooooh, ooooh, ooooh

Upon hearing this, her fellow women would rush to her compound and joined her to shout. Those who came would be rubbed with native chalk (today powder is used). The news of the baby's arrival would be announced to the in-laws and they would fix a date for the birth celebration. The party usually happened during a new moon and the celebration lasted all night. The maternal grandmother would lead the others to the mother-in-law's place with their musical instruments which consisted of Ekwe/Ogene formed from (hollowed log or tree trunk), Udu (clay jug), Opi (flute) and hand bell. They would sing and dance throughout the night while they would be entertained with well-prepared pounded yam and dry fish soup, African salad and fresh palm wine.

As a child, I witnessed several of these ceremonies as I used to accompany my mother sometimes. Today, the birth celebration is no longer celebrated like it used to be, as the child is dedicated in a church ceremony. However, child birth remains a very vital part of any marriage in my community and among Igbo's. Many marriages have failed because the couple could not produce any children. In some cases, because the woman did not bear a male child, the men would marry new wives while the first wife either moved out of the matrimonial home or went back to her family and suffered the ridicule as it was a woman that bore the brunt of a failed marriage in most cases.

Child birth always was a thing of joy for couples and families that were privileged to have a baby especially for the new mother who through childbirth proved she had a fertile womb and thereby stamped her authority and placed her feet strongly in her husband's home and family.

AFTER BIRTH CARE

(Omugwo) is one of the major ceremonies observed in my community and by Igbo's generally after the birth of a child. It was a period meant to take adequate care of the mother. During this time, the nursing mother could recover and replenish her health in order to ensure the optimum production of milk to breastfeed her baby well.

Immediately after delivery, the new mother would be secluded for the *omugwo process*, which is a period during which a woman who had just delivered would be taken care of by her mother, husband and the extended family. Her mother would come over to stay with her during this period or in some cases, the nursing mother would move back in to her maternal home for a time. Zillah, my late elder sister used to come and stay with us after she gave birth to her children. The *Omugwo* process normally would last for three to four weeks. During this period, the nursing mother is petted and her needs adequately attended to.

When I see the way women are treated during the after birth care (Omugwo), I really wished to have been born a woman, but after I witnessed the pain of labor, I would rather remain a man.

A special soup called "ofe nnenwa (baby's mother soup), a special delicacy prepared with spicy leaves, stock fish, dry fish, crayfish and a lot of pepper was prepared for the nursing mother. It was believed that a nursing mother needed a lot of pepper to keep her womb warm. As a child we used to fight over who would get the leftovers from such a delicacy. Fresh palm wine was always available for visitors and the nursing mother who drank sweet and fresh palm wine to enhance the flow of milk for breast feeding her baby.

During such a period the woman regained her strength and replenished the blood lost during the process of childbirth and there evolved a new beauty to the admiration of her husband. When the mother would be at the end of her pampering, she would go home with gifts which she could share with her women friends. The *Omugwo* tradition is still practiced to this date in my community and tribe and remains a strong factor among mothers as it has extended beyond the shores of Igbo land and Nigeria to Europe and America as mothers of expectant women now travel abroad for the Omugwo ritual.

THE BIAFRA WAR BLOOD BATH

" War is delightful to those who have had no experience of it"—Deciderus. I witnessed the Nigeria-Biafra civil war with the eyes of a child but the memories still linger and no cleanser can erase it from my mind. The war which lasted for about three years is a watershed in the history of Nigeria and a big blow to my Igbo tribesmen as no family, village or community in Igbo land escaped from the loss of family members and friends. The devastating effect of the war to the nation, towns, villages and families were great. Every family was given a cup of bitterness and grief.

"The politicians start wars; But ironically, when the war develops and thousands of young soldiers and innocent citizens are killed, it won't be the politicians that brought the war into existence who will die. "If we could read the secret history of our enemies, we should find in each man's life sorrow and suffering enough to disarm any hostility". (Henry Wadsworth Longfellow)

A part of me died in that war. And I wish that it had been the last war. My heart broke when I learnt that my young nephew had enlisted in the American army and was sent to Iraq. Cold shivers ran up and down my spine. I lost my dear uncle Patrick, an uncle who was very fond of me, to the Biafra war. Uncle Patrick was conscripted by the

Biafra soldiers at the heat of the war when the Biafra army and land was caving in to the superior fire power of the Nigerian army and its allies.

The day they came for uncle Patrick, I remember that it was a Sunday and three soldiers came and picked him up from home. He had tried to enlist earlier but was refused at the beginning of the war. Despite his height and athletic build, he was rejected as a soldier recruit. As I was told, initially you needed to know someone in the army or a politician to be recruited. But as the tide turned against Biafra, even children were conscripted into the army. My mother used to carry food to the military base they were camped at before they took Uncle Patrick away.

Men and women both contributed and fought for the Biafra cause. The women would carry food to their sons and relatives at the military base. The old men at home used to comb the bush at night in search of the enemy. No one ever heard from Uncle Patrick again. As a child, I have always thought that he traveled and would return someday but it was later in life that it dawned on me that he indeed travelled but this time, never to return in this lifetime.

"War doesn't determine who is right just who is left" (unknown) My uncle's case was just one case in a million. Along with soldiers who died on the front lines, families at home were wiped out during bomb raids and shelling. Children lost their parents suddenly and parents lost their children, wives lost their husbands and husbands lost their wives. Death was ever near in Biafra land; it knew no limit; was no respecter of persons and claimed unborn children in their mother's womb who never saw the light of day or never felt the warm sunlight on their faces.

Their mothers who would normally keep them safe while in the womb had no means of protection as they were a part of Biafra and were not spared the affront of Nigerian bombs and bullets on the innocent. No place was spared—people died at the market, in church and on their farms as those places were bombed and attacked at will. Those not killed by the bombs and shellfire were killed by hunger, starvation and kwashiorkor, a sickness caused by mal-nutrition during the war. We learnt to take cover in the bush like chickens against the scavenger. We hid in bunkers dug around the bush like rats and rabbits. We ate lizards as meat and raw cassava as food. Everything was edible during war time. Nature was kind to us during this crisis period. Things you would not dream of eating in times of peace, you ate in times of war.

When there is war everyone is out to save their own skin. The war engulfed my community and we evacuated. But where were we running to when the enemy has encircled the whole land? My parents carried a few pieces of luggage and we left with other people heading to no place in particular. Mothers with children tied on their backs, balancing a load upon their heads with the other siblings following behind single file was commonplace. My father carried me on the frame of his bicycle with my legs tied to the frame. Like a lamb meant for sacrifice and with a heavy box at the back, he dragged the bicycle along to no definite destination, but followed along with the throngs of the weary and helpless individuals heading to a destination of fate unknown.

Having been displaced from our homes and communities, we camped as refugees at camouflaged churches and schools. At night we would scramble to find a space to lie on the floor as the hall was full beyond capacity. No day or night passed without people dying in the camp. I remember my parents waking me up from sleep upon discovering that I was sleeping beside a dead woman whom I held onto during sleep thinking it was my mother. The poor woman may have died of hunger and starvation as a total blockade was part of the strategy and weapon the Nigerians applied to annihilate the Biafrans. "The object of war is not to die for your country but to make the other bastard die for his"—General George S. Patton.

Biafran Leader Emeka Ojukwu with Biafra Soldiers
during the War

It takes two to fight and in every war there must be casualties on both sides. Uncle Patrick and the unknown dead woman that lay beside me were victims and casualties of war, they died for Biafra.

Also, to the other side's demise, thousands of young Nigerian soldiers were cut down in the prime of life by the Biafra Ogbunigwe (mass killer), an improvised deadly missile manufactured and used by Biafra in an attempt to annihilate the Nigerian soldiers. They all died for their country. For Nigeria to be one country, it was a task that had to be accomplished by genocide. For Biafra, it was a war for survival and liberty. For me, I side with the philosopher Cicero who said, "There never was a good war, or a bad peace".

War is not good; it has a lot of evil relatives. It destroys life and properties; it retards progress and development, and it introduces crime in society. Once a nation fights a war, it can never be the same again. Forty two years after the Nigerian civil war, the after-effects linger still. One of the worst effects of the war is the rise of armed robbery. Before the war, Nigerians did not know about armed robbers. But after the war armed robbery started and like a hurricane engulfed every part of the country. Armed robbery gave birth to kidnapping and has graduated to a more hydra-like counterpart, terrorism.

Forty two years after, the war bells are ringing again in Nigeria. While the former leader of Biafra and my personal hero, Emeka Odumegwu Ojukwu, (a man I subscribe to for his qualities, ideals and vision for the nation of Nigeria) lays dead and is waiting to be interred to mother earth, the people that started the pogrom and massacre of the Igbo's in 1966 are at it again, through a group that has no love lost for Nigeria and western education which they depict as "evil". The group which has unleashed mayhem in the country has bombed churches where mainly Igbo's were gathered for worship and has ordered Igbo's living in Northern Nigeria to leave. This is a threat that should not be sent off by a wave of hand!

It is far nobler to safeguard life first and foremost, as life imparts meaning and you can restore property you may have lost.

I feel the pain of my kinsmen. I stand for the unity and indivisibility of Nigeria as a nation. But as Malcolm X said, "of what use is it to seek the brotherhood of someone who does not want it". Let peace reign in Nigeria.

PART 2

Education

EDUCATION
AN AWAKENING EXPERIENCE

There is no one without education. It can be formal or informal and each of us acquires some form of education or another in our lifetime.

The informal education is the one received at home where your parents correct you, and teach you how to be an integral part of a family mechanism. Parents who fail to train their children have not taken the mandate of parenthood seriously. My mother was my first educator as it was her job to carry me in utero, to deliver me, to feed and nurse me and to interact and teach me about everyday life.

My formal education started in the seventies after the Biafra war. Parents were approached by teachers to ask if they would send their children back to school. My primary education was as that of a gypsy in that I attended primary school at different places because my village had no school.

Sending a child to school (let alone several children) from the average African family was a very challenging task for poor families and communities. With so many mouths to feed and bodies to clothe, coming up with extra money for school fees was not an easy thing for most parents and many children dropped out of school.

In some families, young girls were subjected to early marriages to alleviate the budget strain on the family. Sometimes we were driven out of school due to fees being unpaid. Credit was non-existent. The poor kids wore shabby school uniforms and many were bare-footed as there was not any money for new uniforms or shoes.

We trekked long distances to attend school in neighboring villages. The school we attended was determined by the number of children eligible for school from each village as we always went in groups.

At one point, I stayed with my married elder sister who lived in another community about 5km from my village. During that period I attended Nenu Community primary school for approximately one session. Among my classmates then were Chisimdi Odingwa and Hon. Eziuche Ubani, a child who later became a journalist, politician and member of the Nigeria legislature.

Among the teachers I remember in that school were sir Njoku, a man with glaring red eyes and a former Biafra soldier. The other noteworthy teacher was sir Ogbonna. Both men were known for their tough disciplinary measures. I also attended Ohuhu Ekwuru primary school—a school in another neighboring village. I remember madam Ezengwa, my first teacher in primary level 1 and the headmaster who was nicknamed sir Odim uto (meaning it sweets me). This name came about because when he was flogging scholars, he would make sure that you enjoyed the stroke of his cane that graced your buttocks. We were always scared of him. I remember how we used to go and fetch firewood for him and how scared we would be to deliver the wood to his home. As the fear of sir Odim was the beginning of wisdom for every scholar in that school.

I later changed to the Amaisii community primary school in Mgbokonta where I completed my primary education. I remember the high standard of learning and education we had in primary school. The morning devotion before classes was something to look forward to. The teachers would arrange us up in a queue, according to classes and we marched like soldiers in a parade to the sound of the school band. At the prompt of the band boys and the school master who was on the side giving orders, you would hear songs like;

> "Nigeria is a land of great liberty
> Great liberty, great liberty
> Nigeria is a land of great liberty
> And some of you know it well
> Oh Niger" . . .

> "Oo my home Oo my home
> Oo my home Oo my home
> When shall I see my home?
> Oo my home
> When shall I see my native land?
> I will never forget my home".

With these motivating songs we marched in to the main school hall for morning devotion. During the devotion, we sang more songs, and two or three scholars that had learnt poems and recitations were called to deliver their memorized poems and recitations before the full hall with all eyes and attention focused on the person. Sometimes the student faltered in his recitation due to stage fright and would quit halfway through. The successful ones would receive hand clapping according to the order of the school master. That used to encourage others to learn at home. Also we would sing the old Nigerian National anthem during the morning devotion.

> "Nigeria, we hail thee, our own dear native land,
> Though tribe and tongue may differ,
> In brotherhood we stand,
> Nigerians all are proud to serve our sovereign motherland . . ."

This was Nigeria's National anthem from 1960 to 1978. I sang it last in the seventies during my primary school days. That was a way of showing the spirit of patriotism and love for the motherland in us. I remember it was in such occasion that my school mate, Chidi Ikpeama recited a short poem which stuck to my memory until today. The poem was,

> "I have seen a scene
> In the scene of river sin
> Where a mother can murder her own child".

With the methods our teachers taught us, I developed an interest in poetry and literature at an early stage and started writing and composing poems from class one in college. Among the schools attended up to this stage,

Amaisii primary school Mgbokonta impacted me most. There were very intelligent boys and girls in school and there was very stiff competition for the top spots in the ranking of exams.

Also this is where I met Chisom (late), Amadi, and Nkasi (late) who were my childhood friends. Because we were very little and young and there were adults in our class, our teacher always gave us seats in the front row. There were mature boys and girls, some in their late twenties and thirties still in primary school. And we the younger ones were bullied by them. Therefore the three of us were always close and together and we stood our ground to fight and defend ourselves from any bully.

Madame Ihesiulo was one of my favourite teachers. She was very nice and fond of me because of my skill in telling short stories, poems, and Bible recitations. She was proficient at her work, and had the candor to express her mind. Like a good shepherd she would go looking for any of her sheep who were not present and accounted for. I will never forget the day she came looking for me at home due to my absence from school for a period due to ill-health. When she arrived, I was outside playing football with an orange in the sand with other children. Of course I was half naked and not in uniform.

She fondly called to me, "Onuoha, Onuoha," and it was like God calling Adam in the Garden of Eden. Once I noticed her, I ran away with my heels almost touching my neck. I felt ashamed to stand before a female teacher half naked so my gut reaction was to run from her. She was a teacher who really cared for her wards. Many years have elapsed since I saw her last but I will always remember her as one who helped to direct me towards the right path to follow at the tender age in life. "A hen never forgets who plucked her feathers during rainy season", (African proverb).

Also, I remember headmaster Nwagbara whose notable characteristic in my juvenile mind was how his nose discharged cigarette smoke like the exhaust pipe of his rickety Volkswagen Beetle car. He was a terror to us as everyone was afraid of him because of the way he flogged school children mercilessly. He would walk into class to teach the principles of agriculture carrying bundles of cane in both hands. He would ask, "If a plant or animal dies and decays, what would it add to the soil?" He would not waste time to say "you, you and you" with his bundles of cane pointing at the ignorant scholars, and if you did not provide the answer immediately, his bundle of cane would descend on you at the speed of light and he would scream, "humus!"

The standard of education was high and we were taught about personal hygiene as the teachers used to inspect our teeth and nails and if they were found to be dirty, you would be punished. Also we learnt things about the world in general studies and geography. We knew about the seven continents of the world. We learned about Africa's seven major rivers in song: Nile, Niger, Senegal, Congo, Orange, Limpopo and Zambezi.

We were taught about rivers outside of Africa: the Mississippi and Amazon to name a few. We explored the textbooks which told of the major rivers in Africa and other parts of the globe and about the biggest mountains in Africa and beyond—Mount Kilimanjaro, Futa Jalon, and Ararat to name a few. It has never ceased to amaze and surprise me now when an adult in Europe asks me a question such as, "is Africa in Nigeria?" I shake my head and I wonder if his teacher did not teach him the difference between a country and a continent while in primary school.

CHILDREN AND
INDEPENDENCE DAY

C hildren's Day is May 27 and Nigerian Independence Day is a holiday on October 1st. These two days were very important days during my primary school years as the primary and college students celebrated these two events with a military parade type of competition. This was a delight to watch as the children from various schools gathered at the zonal headquarters to perform the parade competition.

The teachers would drill us and we practiced for many days before the main event. The best students among the boys and girls were selected to represent the school while the rest of us would cheer them on. As there were no vehicles to transport us to the match site, we usually would leave early in the morning and in a two-wheeled convoy of bicycles we rode the 8-10 kilometers to the headquarters where the competition was being held.

It was a colorful celebration featuring the military band that supplied heart-pumping music for the parade while the children marched past in time to the rhythm, swinging their arms left and right. As they approached the podium where the Governor's representatives were standing, the children would turn their heads towards the podium to salute the officials. The Boy Scouts, Boy's Brigade, Girls

Guides, Junior Missionary Volunteers, Red Cross and college students would also parade across in an attractive formation. The best schools were judged on their marching formation and awarded prizes at the end of the ceremonies. This event was scheduled a few days before the last day of the school session.

The last day of school and the long vacation that followed our promotion to a higher class was always memorable. It would always be a day of mixed feelings for many children as those who passed the examinmation would be promoted to a new class, while those that failed would repeat the class. On this day the promotion examination results were read and a type of mini-graduation was held for the students graduating from one level to the next level. Parents and older siblings back from college would attend this ceremony with all of its pomp and circumstance. They would come fashionably dressed and rejoiced as the results were read. The presence of these college students used to inspire and motivate me to study harder as I wished to be like them some day.

COLLEGE EDUCATION

I entered secondary school (college as we call it in Nigeria) in 1977 at about the age of ten after passing the common entrance and the school leaving certificate examinations. Passing the common entrance was very difficult. Eight of us from the school passed the exam that year and four of us from the same school, Chisom (late) Theophilus, and Princewill who later became my close friends and classmates were posted to the Anglican Boys Grammar School Nbawsi. Leaving home and parents for the first time to live in a boarding situation far from home was not an easy transition.

Even at my tender age, my concern was for my parents and how they would cope as two of my elder siblings, Sarah and Fineboy were already in college; my eldest brother Josiah was learning a trade, and my younger siblings Oluchi and Glory were in primary school. What an added burden and vacuum my leaving home would create, as I had become very useful, helpful and supportive to them in the absence of my elder siblings.

I am sure they considered all the options and indeed found my leaving very difficult as well, but despite the difficulties, a college education was something I had dreamed of and I too wished to acquire higher learning and be on the receiving end of the seeming respect accorded to college students. Moreover, I wanted to experience the college life that Fineboy my brother used to tell me about. I wanted to dance disco, a special privilege college students used to enjoy during vacations. On such occasions they used to cover the half-walls of the school hall with fresh palm fronds to ward off peeping eyes, and unauthorized entrants. However we used to play peeping eyes by peering through the tiny openings on the palm covered upper walls. As a school boy I have always wished to partake in that type of dancing someday.

The day of departure came, and I left my home wearing my college uniform which consisted of black knickers, a white shirt and my Cortina sandal shoe. I carried my metal school box close to my side and Father and I were off to my new school. It was an emotional scene saying goodbye as I remember my mother and younger sisters bursting into tears as we boarded the vehicle that conveyed us to the school about 20 kilometers from home. I was deeply touched that my mother shed tears while I was waving goodbye to relatives who were wishing me well and waving in return. That was my first time riding in a car. I was startled and amazed by the scenery outside the car window that appeared as though the grass and trees were running alongside the vehicle.

As we arrived at the school gate and while undergoing the clearance process, three senior students rushed over to us. One of them hurriedly collected my luggage and asked me to follow him. He introduced himself as John Echeji, a boy who later became my school master. Father reminded me to be a good boy and then he left. From there, the journey into a new life, a new path, and a new world began for me. It was a path that would define, develop and put me on track towards the route and course to steer the ship of my life. I had just been born once again into a new family, village and community where my teachers were my parents and my fellow students were my brothers. I had begun a journey to acquire education and knowledge that would impact and change my life. It was a pathway where the ground was level for the children of the rich and poor as they would sleep under the same roof, as well as eat from the same pot. Here family background and parental upbringing were put to the test. It was an environment where bad association could corrupt good manners and bad manners were amended also. And I resolved that if it was going to be, it was up to me.

On the first day, I felt so lost; the environment was new and so strange to me. There were beautiful lawns with Melina trees, pathways lined with whistling pines, buildings comprised of hostels, academic blocks, a laboratory, a library, teacher's quarters and more. I felt so out of place in a foreign environment until I met up with the three boys from my former primary school. They had started at this school a term before me. I followed them wherever they went and we were always together.

My bliss of newfound companions was turned upside down very quickly by my first baptism of fire. One senior Nnadozie, (you dare not call a senior student by name without attaching the prefix of "senior" to it) who was a class two student and notorious for his use of ambiguous words and grammar commanded me to come back towards him as we walked past each other. He pointedly asked me who I was and which class I belonged to, and I responded with my name and class. Immediately he shouted, "You fox, why did you touch me with your tail? Must you kneel down?" Of course as a new student at a lower level, you did not argue but did as they commanded.

While I was kneeling down two of his friends came and asked what happened. His answer was, "Imagine this fox, bedraggled me with his dirty tail!" "What an abomination," his friend exclaimed. "Come on, lie down!" Nnadozie ordered. "Who gave you the impudence, audacity and temerity to touch an erudite scholar slovenly with your tail?" To which I whispered, "But senior, I have no tail." "Shaaaarrrrrrrp, imagine . . . An imp, a lout, with your acrid odor trying to snaffle with my candor" was the comeback response. Stupefied by his vocabulary, I thought to myself that college must be the seat of all knowledge as I have never heard such grammar before. It didn't make sense, but I was impressed!

I kept lying down until a class four student who saw what was going on came and rescued me. After that episode, I started getting used to incessant punishment from senior students, especially the class two students who were a thorn in the flesh of class one students. Two days after my father took me to the school, I returned home as I could not stay behind alone when my three friends went home instead of going to the Independence Day celebrations.

My parents were surprised to see me back at home. Mother had sympathy for me after I narrated my ordeal in the hands of senior students and my experience for the two days spent at college. Father was not happy that I came back so soon. He encouraged me to go back and face my college education bravely like so many other students had in the past. And in his inimitable way, father wisely pointed out that the senior students also passed through the same experience as class one students. After my short return home and after other various incidents, I resolved to face the challenges ahead of me in college.

The college had six dormitories for students: Ibiam house, Dimeari, Okonkwo, Okwuosa, Nwachukwu and New house. I was in Ibiam house and lived in the dormitory along with the prefect assigned to me and the other boys. Prefects were senior students appointed as heads by the school authorities to take charge of fellow students and assume supervision of the ones in their charge.

College photo, Author squating 2nd from left front row

Echehi, my school master was newly appointed the school's light prefect, as he was in charge of the big generator that supplies light in the school. And serving a prefect's boy had some privileges: it protected you from incessant punishment and bullying from senior students as your other colleagues were prone to, it absolved you from having to fetch water for the refectory and it saved you from washing the plates of the other senior students. On occasion, you had the opportunity to enjoy extra food from your master's dish as prefects had the privilege of having seconds of everything during meal time. Unfortunately, I never got to enjoy any of the second helpings as my master had a large stomach and hardly left anything on his plate. My college being an all-boys school had many big boys who were Biafra soldiers at one time. Sometimes you felt as if you were in a military school. And the younger and junior students sometimes suffered bullying from the mature students.

WELCOMING THE NEW STUDENTS

The first social gathering I attended at college was the annual welcome ceremony for new students. This was the day we were officially born into and admitted to the school. The whole student-body gathered at the school main hall together with the teachers, and the principal, I. Nwandu. With his well-tailored black suit and a nice haircut complete with a part to one side, the principal stood out like he was the President or some elite Head of State among the rest of the school staff and prefects accompanying him.

The principal commanded an overwhelming influence on the students and some said he used charm. He addressed the students and highlighted the rules and regulations of the school and the need for us to take our studies seriously. After the principal left, Friday Apollos, a much-feared by the students senior prefect, stepped up to address the students and emphasized that no act of insolence or disobedience would be tolerated from any student.

The most remarkable event of the day for me was the ballroom dance in the evening where the hall was full of students both old and new, and the students danced to sweet meaningful reggae songs. Class one students were asked to dance alone, and many felt so shy to take the dance floor, but they were forced to do so. I remember dancing to the sweet lyrics of Eric Donaldson's, "The land of my birth", Sweet Breeze's, "Palm wine the tapper remember me" and Jimmy Cliff, "You can get it if you really want"—songs that motivated, inspired and stuck in my heart so much. These were the songs of my time, these were days when music had messages that touched the heart and I danced to the music of my era. I danced to the admiration of many senior students. And from then on many senior students came to like me.

THE SCHOOL CLUBS, SPORTS
AND GAMES

As students we participated in extracurricular activities. We had various clubs like the Scripture Union, Martial Arts, the Red Cross, Boy Scouts, and Press Club among others. I belonged to the press club because of my love for writing. While in class one, I used to compose and write letters for some classmates to send home to their parents or to their friends. The press club was like the college watch dog. We posted articles and cartoons on the school's notice board.

The club helped us to develop our writing skills. Some of my mates from the press club are now top press men and media practitioners in Nigeria and abroad. A person like the Honorable Eziuche Ubani eventually became the press secretary to the former president in the Nigeria's House of Representatives and is presently a legislator in the same house and Andy Ekugo who has been one of the editors in This Day newspaper began in press club and rose to great heights in the media world.

The college institution served as a veritable birthing ground for students to develop their talents and from that ground came great athletes, sportsmen and football players (soccer to you North Americans). My school participated in various games and sporting competitions such as tennis, javelin, jumping, and football to name a few. We had inter-house sports, inter-college sports and football competitions both on state and national levels. I liked football most and I played in my school's Mosquito team as it was the list category for young boys. I remember some students who distinguished themselves in sports and games. People like Kobrete Charles who was the best in 800 meters dash and represented the school and State in national competitions, Kingsley Nworisa, a very good boxer, and Anthony Eguzo one of the best football players the school produced.

JUVENILE DELIQUENCY

Despite the high level of discipline and good morals the teachers tried to impart in us, it was difficult to avoid peer pressure and I fell into the abyss of behaviors contrary to the school rules and regulations. Many of us took to smoking and drinking, jiving and clubbing, dabbling in the occult, and many other vices. I was caught in the web of rebellion and started smoking cigarettes around the age of 12 and studying in the class two level. It was a way of beefing up my social status. I probed the folly in those vices so that none would be new to me later in life. I was very popular and mixed with some known bad boys and seniors much older than me. Of course, I was very careful never to let my parents catch on as that would have been the end of my moonlighting career.

We gave ourselves nicknames. We had names like Corruption, Viper, Rasta, Jew man, No two ways, Man die go, and Movement among others. I was called Movement, a name that has followed me up to the present day. Sometimes you are inclined to behave like the name you bear. I was always on the move, travelling from one place to another, even my style of walking changed with the inception of the name. Many students were carried away by some of these indulgences and became dropouts. Some finished school and unfortunately proceeded into the larger world of corruption and its practices.

Despite peer group pressure in college, I never allowed myself to go overboard as I was always guided by the biblical principles my parents taught me. The training I received as a child was like a string on my waist always pulling me back even up to the present day!

"Train up a child in the way he should go: and when he is old, he will not depart from it". **Proverbs 22:6 Holy Bible** King James Version (KJV)

MY MENTORS

The best way to success is to follow the footsteps of those who have journeyed before us. My major mentor in life has been God as my faith in Him has always waxed strong. I have endeavored to always put Him first in whatever I do. Beyond my relationship with God, my only mentor is self. I have always befriended myself and have never allowed anything to stop me half way as I wouldn't let my parents down lest their efforts be in vain. I know that if it's going to be, it depends on me. I never belittle or write myself off in anything. Even when I fail, I feel spurred on to continue and succeed. Having no affluent family background was a kind of motivating factor to strive to succeed and re-invent my world.

Although I see myself as my mentor, I would fail greatly if I did not pay homage to my parents and family background. Some remarkable people have traveled through my life. My older sister Sarah and her husband Tony Ajiere have always served as good mentors for me. Sarah's life and her life's experiences were like Sarah of the Bible. In marriage she rejected all the people that would come courting and the raves of the moment and settled for a man who was yet to find his feet. They faced a great deal of challenges after marriage, but always together as one, they forged ahead.

Sarah's strong faith in God has seen her through as well as her astute qualities in resource management and ideas. Tony's unequaled fighting spirit and dogged determination surmounting all obstacles to rise from nothing to something above his equals spurred him on. I have been astounded and amazed by their progress through life's hills and valleys and even now, I remain a fan.

Among some of the other people who have profoundly touched my life is Heart Emerole, the first person from my village to study abroad, and the first elite my village produced. He was a principal and educator. I always admired the standard of living and quality of training he gave his children and family. Some of my favorite writers and authors have greatly influenced me. As I read Chinua Achebe's books, I wish I could write like him or even better. I heard stories about Zik of Africa and his exploits as a journalist and writer and I became much more motivated. His achievements have always goaded me. Also among my mentors include my college principal I. Nwandu who would always encourage us to study hard as to be leaders of tomorrow.

With the realization that I have always liked and have had a penchant for stories and writing, and with the realization that all my mentors excelled through education, hard work and self-determination, I therefore decided that I must obtain a university education as to enable me achieve my goal. "Really great people make you feel that you, too, can become great". Mark Twain quotes. (American Humorist, Writer and Lecturer. 1835-1910). Anything that has a beginning must have an end. I completed my college education successfully and was ready to step into the world.

The college education was a stepping stone to stir up self-knowledge and awareness to soar to greater heights in life. I learned much, and that knowledge propelled me forward. I now had information about the 19th century colonization of Africa by the white man and how he perceived the black race as servile and inferior. I also learned how some of the missionaries were false messengers who came as snakes with a bible in one hand to supposedly evangelize us when in reality they used it as a cover to aid and abet the others of their race who were there to invade and exploit Africa's human and natural resources. With the good friends I met and exposure to information about the world and other continents I too wanted to change the world. Indeed I was packaged to step into the larger world.

Despite the hardships encountered, the youthful exuberances, as well as the adventures and fun we had, I would say that my college days were the most pleasant and memorable days of my life. And I wish I could go back to those days and relive them once more. But now, I can only say, "Oh happy days come back to me." And I wish the happy moments would come back to me again, but as we know, it is never as it was and memory is the best place to relive those days.

GOING INTO THE LARGER WORLD

"The desire to get ahead is a compelling fashion in today's world". Dr. Myles Muroe. (The Bahamas Faith Ministries International BFMI). www.wikipedia. org. Graduating from college in 1982, like most young men fresh out of school, I believed I could take the bull by the horns and conquer the world. Nothing was insurmountable. There comes a time in the life of a man when you are no longer tied to the apron strings of parents or society; a time you break loose and go for independence, and take the driver's seat of your life and make your own life decisions.

Though I had my dreams and goals to pursue a university education, I could not proceed further to university due to lack of funds and sponsorship. I thought about the possibilities of getting a job in the highly saturated and competitive Nigerian job market but after weighing my options, I decided to do a vocational training course on architecture and engineering draftsmanship. Armed with that, I reasoned it would be easier for me to create a job and employment for myself and make money to further my education.

After I qualified as a draftsman, I worked as an architectural draftsman and project supervisor for architectural firms and later as a pipeline engineering draftsman in some of the oil servicing companies. As custom demands, I remember taking the first money I earned to my parents who blessed me and prayed for my greater success. After a few years of practice, I bought my first car, a Volkswagen and later a Mercedes Benz. I have always wanted to be my own boss—an employer and entrepreneur rather than an employee. After working for some companies I decided to float my own private company and I established my own firm which offered building design, auto cad, as well as construction and contract services. I was awarded some very notable and large projects by my clients.

I have always placed a great deal of importance on education and had always had the vision to further my education at the university level in order to enable me to learn more and excel in life. In 1995, I gained admission to study mass communications in university as I have always been convinced that my true profession and calling was that of journalism and writing as most of my mentors were journalists and writers. When I was in college, I had the reputation of being a writer and novelist.

Journalists and novelist are entrusted with a great charge: that of balancing truth and popular opinion in the society. This is a more relevant profession for me because it offers a larger spectrum and platform for me to contribute to national and international issues. For me the journalism profession and writing is like priesthood, where you have to be called and anointed like the high priest in the old testament of the bible. And I believe I was called and anointed right from the womb to shine the light for others to see.

My innate desire not to settle for the good in the here and now when my conviction has always been that I can get the best in the future made me abandon my university degree program in the final year when I took a leap abroad to search for greener pastures. But of course, the pastures are never quite as green, in fact sometimes when examined close up the pasture is littered with gravel and green weeds. As I was not satisfied with what I have achieved or where I was in life, the realization became that I needed to go back to university and acquire a university degree.

PART 3

Striking Memories
in My Childhood and Life

Life is a journey, and I am a traveler, and my people said that a traveler must eat unripe plantain. Life's journey is not that smooth. The road is rough and thorny, and is filled with scorpions and lions. Sometimes you stumble and fail, you are pierced, you might receive painful bites and are scared witless by certain events of surprise, but you don't look back. Despite the odds, pain and fears, I keep moving on.

THE DEATH OF MY SISTERS

Death has always been a bitter pill everyone must one day swallow. Memories of certain incidents in life are cruel and upsetting to relive. They are better forgotten but sorrow from losing a dear one never goes away. It is said that time is the healer of physical, psychological and emotional injuries, but the loss of my four sisters is a torture I have to bear for life. The two younger sisters, Ngozi and Philistia died when I hardly knew them. My two elder sisters, Chioma and Zillah are a loss that I fail to put into words.

The irony of it all is that both Chioma and Zillah died during child delivery because of the lack of medical care in my community. Chioma died sometime in 1970 after the civil war. I used to live with her as her home was just a stone's throw from my parent's home. She was such a beautiful lady and bore a real resemblance to my mother. It's painful that she died in the very natural process of childbirth due to complications and the lack of a basic health care system.

The year 1985 proved to be a cruel year for me and my family. My sister Zillah was the first daughter and eldest sister to us all and was like a second mother to us. She used to be a rallying point as we always obtained most useful advice from her. I learnt she was such a brilliant student during her school days. But all those qualities were cut short by death. She died while giving birth for the tenth time, and this time it was a set of twins. The news about her death was so shocking to me and the family. The whole village went berserk with grief on the event of her death. My mother was uncontrollable with sorrow. I could not bear it either; I wept. It was one death that really touched me deeply. It's hard to recover from this kind of sorrow and I dedicate this composition to my departed sister.

TO A DEPARTED SISTER

Many years ago you left
The clutch hands of death
Could not allow you
To leave a word for your loved ones
Your departure was painful
You entered the way of womanhood
But could not come out of it
You paid the price of the curse
Laid on the proto woman
You departed in pain and sorrow

The seed of the woman you labored
To bring to the world
Rather than come with you
Or go back alone
Preferred to take you
To the world beyond
There was pandemonium
On the eve of your departure
The entire village was shaken
On hearing the news

To some it sounded like a tell—tale
Your age mates never believed
The family went berserk with sorrow
To others it was like a bad dream
That later became a reality
What a surge of uncontrollable tears
Before passing on you had wished
To speak to mother
But the death messenger
Jealous of your beauty
Was in a hurry to take you away

And he never waited for her to arrive
You resisted leaving
But you were under the grip of a colossus
Like an obedient child you obeyed
And dropped the last breadth
Your remains were laid in the family hut
Many years have gone by now
Yet no memorial for you
No epitaph was written on your grave
No wreath was lead

No picture to behold your charming beauty
Though in mother lies your portrait
For you were her images
But in me remain your pigments
The glimpse of your charming beauty
Caught with my infant eyes
Remains evergreen
You were caring and tenderly
I wished you had left behind
A living image of yourself

The man you shared your life with
Has lost memory of you
Beclouded with a new vow
To a second comer
Has forgotten his first love
Men sometimes for passion
Forget the dead
Never mind out of many souls
You are remembered by one
Your name remains in the family tree
And will pass over to later generation

Could the dead be given a little time off?
To visit the land of the living
You will be amazed with the changes
And developments that have taken place
I am now a young man
No longer the snotty toddler

Frolicking on sand
You used to know
I am at the noon of life
Papa has gone
And mama has far gone the evening

They were father and mother to you here
But son and daughter
To be to you hereafter
And their younger brother would I be
When life's metamorphosis
has run its course on us
If the departed are happy where they are
Happy you may be
And happier we would be
When later we meet again.

MY MISSING RIB

"Whoso findeth a wife findeth a good thing, and obtaineth favour of the Lord." Proverbs 18:22 (King James Version of the Holy Scriptures). Looking for a wife and marriage is one of the most pleasant memories in a man's life. And I believe marrying the right partner is the best thing that could happen to any man or woman. For me the road to marriage was a long journey and delayed due to going abroad. Before I found my wife, I fell in love a few times and while they could have been good marriages, they would not have been what I have today. I remember one in particular—she was a girl whom I thought I would have married but she later married another man.

In the novel African Night Entertainment, the author writes "women are like clothes in a market place, the first to price it may not be the buyer". Cyprian Ekwensi. Marriage is an adventure and a leap into the unknown and indeed it is bliss if one finds his real missing rib.

My marriage was an act of risk because I never knew or met the girl I was marrying before paying the bride price. I did not have to fill anybody's yam barns, or pay in goats and chickens, as we were well beyond the village with me living in Madrid, Spain while my wife was in Lagos, Nigeria. I was acquainted with a cousin of hers who spoke very highly of a wonderful lady named Anthonia. I took the cousin's word to heart and did not waste any time in contacting her. The first thing that struck me was her voice. It was like a balm and a soothing ointment to my soul.

The sweetness of her voice could disarm and melt the heart of the worst terrorist. A friend who happened to be in Nigeria went to see her on my behalf and upon doing so, gave a good report and encouraged me to go and pay her dowry the next day without any delay. We exchanged pictures, and I found her very delightful. We courted through telephone calls and through emails. Of course, I had to inform my family members. But the question always asked was, "have you met her? How could you marry someone you never met?" For me the oddity of this process was the clincher, as what may seem odd to others catches my interest. It has always been so. Life is a script, a script in which we have the privilege and liberty of deciding which characters we want to play.

In 2007, I made a leap into the unknown of marriage and it was indeed blissful and continues to be. The first time I met my wife upon arriving at the airport was like a dream sequence from a film. The marriage date and arrangements had been scheduled and made before my arrival. On the arrival date, my wife was supposed to be at the airport to welcome me. We only knew each other through photos and I had her photo in my pocket but as I quickly found out, sometimes pictures do not tell the full story.

Upon coming out to the arrival lounge, I expected the first person to meet me would be my Anthonia. It was no surprise that I presumed the lady standing with my friend who gave me the go-ahead on securing Anthonia as my wife would be my beloved—she who had won my heart. In the spirit of love and passion for my betrothed, I grabbed her to myself and kissed her warmly. She did not resist as she responded in kind. I held on to her for a bit as I was sure she was the one I would pledge my love to, but as it turned out, she was not the one I came for, but rather my friend's fiancée.

Needless to say, the family onlookers stared at me in unbelief and amazement. My wife's elder sister and my friend tried their best to get my attention and questioned me with, "don't you know your wife?" I was quite startled by it all and quickly asked "is this not my wife?" while dis-engaging from the lady I had just locked lips with. I became confused, and there was much drama. It was then I realized that the lady was not my wife but my friend's fiancée. My wife was standing to the side watching calmly. On recognizing my real wife, I rushed and grabbed her to kiss her passionately. I thought perhaps I had been set up as a joke, but a very bad joke at that. My poor wife on her own part was equally confused as she thought that perhaps I was not who I said I was over the courtship, or that perhaps I may have changed my mind. After the airport drama was sorted out, I thought perhaps I could relax, but there was an even bigger shock awaiting me.

The traditional tribal marriage and church wedding were fixed on the same day due to time constraints. On the wedding day, I was on my way to the ceremony when I received a call from my wife; she was hysterically sobbing on the phone and relayed the news that the priest had cancelled the wedding. I wondered how the priest could arbitrarily spoil our day. I resolved within me that there was no going back. If the priest for any reason decided not to wed us, we could go on with the traditional marriage and have the church wedding at another time and place.

Precious and the Wife

Precious and the Family

According to the priest, the reason for cancelling the wedding was because people living abroad sometimes marry someone from the country they live in and then go to Nigeria to marry another Nigerian and in essence they commit bigamy. Therefore since the priest was not sure whether I was in that category, he had to postpone the wedding. Since I knew I was free of such commitment, I left him to absolve his mind from all doubts while the traditional marriage went on.

Marriage is like a package, you never know the contents until you open it. Despite the initial doubts and fears regarding the circumstances in which we met, we have found our missing ribs in each other. She is exactly what I wanted: someone respectful to her husband and a good companion.

Our marriage has been successful and we have been blessed with a child. With experiences involving my wife, my mother and my elder sister (Sara), I am passionate about women and the family system and the unique role women play in establishing the home. The reality of a home is the woman. The stress and troubles that women go through to maintain their marriage and home is highly commendable. I appreciate the diligence of women. "A home without a woman is like a barn without cattle."(African proverb)

PART 4

Travels, Experiences Living in Europe. A Balance Between the Past and Present

LEAVING THE HOMELAND

Many factors compel individuals to leave their homeland. To some it may be because of war, insecurity, persecution, violence, poverty or for socio-economic reasons ... In my own case, I should say it was by choice and for reasons of personal convenience and not out of absolute necessity considering my status at the time I left. In my life I have always longed to break away from the curse of generational and situational poverty. Generational poverty according to Ruby K. Payne, PhD, www.gazettextra.com is being in poverty for two generations. While situational poverty is a shorter time and is caused by circumstance e.g. deaths, illness, divorce, war, etc. not excluding ignorance and lack of education.

Passion and significance for success compelled me to leave the homeland. And it was also the same passion that led some great men and women, including the founding fathers of the United States of America, to sacrifice their families, friends, and home land to journey to an unknown country, far removed from what they knew. My aim has always been to lift my family across the poverty line to the other side of the economic class, and to end the situational poverty circle for my children. It is the wish of every good parent for their children to be better off than they were. Also I left home to satisfy my curiosity to know more about the world outside of my sphere of knowledge. I was motivated by the desire to acquire the Golden Fleece and the greener pasture that I was brainwashed to believe that Europe and America offered.

I also needed to delve into the myths of the white man for myself and to determine whether popular opinion about the white man was indeed fact. While in school, I learnt about slave trade, how the black man (Negroes) were taken as slaves to work at farms in Europe and the new world, (America). I also learned that after massive slavery of the Black man, the white imperialists from Europe and America colonized the African continent.

As an inquisitive sort, I wanted to know about the perceived superiority of the white race over the black race. I wanted to investigate the notion of the white man's concept that the black man is savage and servile. I wanted to know more about the fantastic stories and impressions given about Europe and America as a paradise on earth by those who had been there. This is what motivated me to take a leave from my homeland and seek out adventure abroad to the white man's land.

"What you think about the most or focus on the most is what will appear as your life" T. Harv Eker. Secrets of the Millionaire Mind (Harper Business an Imprint of Harper Collins Publishers). www.harpercollins.com. Coming to Europe was not a dream but a vision. I don't put much stock in dreams but firmly believe in vision as dreams are cloudy and sometimes vanish. Vision remains and keeps you focused and established on the path at hand. Therefore after my college education, when I started working and living on my own, my interest and attention always inclined me to garner foreign information and newsfeeds from Europe and America. I sought after employment in multi-national companies and interacted with the expatriate staff. The first two attempts made to travel failed and I lost my resources, but I never lost my vision or relentlessness. Purpose always sets a course after determining the end and encourages the traveler along the way.

My architectural and contracting services had started thriving as I started handling contracts worth large amounts of money. I also made some investments at home. At this time I thought that the right time had come for me to realize my vision and I set out for it. I kept my plans to myself and never shared it with my family members. The idea was that if it did not work, no one would know, and no one would feel sorry for me as I detest pity. If I failed, I would just continue with my normal activity.

It is said that life is a shooting range so never miss your target. I left Nigeria and went to the Benin republic to process my visa to Europe through the assistance of my cousin living there. "Ask, and it shall be given you; seek, and ye shall find; knock, and it shall be opened unto you: Mathew 7: 7 Holy Bible King James Version (KJV). With that biblical injunction in mind, I asked, sought and knocked at the door of the Dutch embassy and the door of Europe was opened for me with a visa to Germany. I never returned home again to bid farewell to my parents and family. A day before my departure I informed my elder sister Sarah on the phone that I would be leaving for Germany. She was surprised, though happy and she wasted no time in scolding me for not saying my proper goodbyes. My philosophy is that life is an adventure, and from there I took a leap into the unknown.

MEMORIES OF GERMANY

I arrived in Germany in 2001. It was at the thick of the winter period. As I landed at the airport, the reality of leaving home and a familiar environment to a strange land, people, language and culture dawned on me. Everywhere I looked I saw white faces and pointed noses. It reminded me of the story I was told about two kinsmen, Mba and Avoaja who went to a job interview where they were seeking a painter. Mba was the successful candidate while Avoaja was rejected because he was so taken by the Englishman's pointed nose rather than concentrating on the purpose of the interview.

The Englishman asked Mba his experience in painting. Mba described and demonstrated how they used clay mixed in water to paint their mud houses. While Mba was trying to prove his experience, Avoaja was contemplating the Englishman's pointed nose and other features. The Englishman noticed that Avoaja was not serious about what he had come for, and said to him," Mr. Avoaja, that which you are looking for you will not get it".

Therefore, I did not allow myself to be scared of the faces and pointed noses I saw and this would not interfere with my goals. In Nigeria there is a good sized community of white people and I interacted and worked with them but I had never been in the midst of a white multitude like this before. I was in the company of my cousin (a very fair skinned black man) and I was the odd man out in a predominantly white society with being as black as I am. My cousin is like a mulatto, (fair skinned) or what Nigerians call 'unfortunate European" and the German eyes kept following me wherever I went. I said to myself "be a man, despite their colors they are human beings and no man is foreign to me."

We passed through the immigration protocols and took a train to Duisburg to meet my cousin's friend Oti, who came to meet us. While on the train to Duisburg, my thoughts went back to Nigeria. I remembered the last time I had a train ride. Back in the 70's during my college days we used to travel from school to some cities on the train with cheap fares. The train was also very useful to the rural dwellers for transporting food items to the cities. Today rail transport has been abandoned for years in Nigeria and is no longer functioning due to bad governance. My first train ride upon my arrival to Germany gave me an idea of what a good train system should be like. The stations had electronic ticket machines and inside the train were very neat and comfortable seats for passengers and one could stay abreast of the news while riding as televisions were mounted in each coach.

As we came down from the train at the station and walked towards Oti's house I saw very fine and modern busses stopped at the bus stops with people boarding in an orderly fashion without rushing or pushing. And to my surprise the drivers were neatly dressed in their suits and ties. I wondered whether this was reality as it was such a stark contrast with the Lagos bus stops where passengers and bus drivers are pushed and pulled like cattle. A typical Lagos bus hardly stops for passengers. At the bus stops it slows down only for passengers to jump out and jump in while the conductor shouts himself hoarse announcing routes and destinations. It used to be survival of the fittest to board a bus in Lagos. As we walked along, I noticed that the buildings, though not fantastic in terms of architectural aesthetics, were uniformly patterned and nicely spaced with beautiful flowers, well-manicured lawns, and eye-pleasing landscaping.

The road network was very good with visible vertical and horizontal road signs, traffic lights, and neat walkways and bicycle lanes. I saw people kissing openly on the road and in public places—something unusual to me, but normal in this part of the world as I later realized. There were numerous men and women strolling along with well-dressed dogs on their leashes. People give very tender care and attention to the dogs here in Europe—another custom quite unfamiliar to me.

With what I observed in a short time on the journey from the airport to Oti's place, I knew that I was in a new and different environment and a world far from home. I noticed a sense of orderliness, discipline and a kind of organized system in this part of the world compared to Lagos as Nigeria's biggest city and the first port of call to most visitors and foreigners coming to Nigeria. Life in

Lagos is far from normal. It is said that every other city in Nigeria has a "Welcome" sign except Lagos. I told myself, from now on it's no more Lagos or Nigeria life, but rather I would take the German life.

I was amazed by the lights that beamed both day and night without any electrical failures during my stay in Germany. This was rather an unusual experience compared to Lagos and other cities back home in Nigeria where there isn't a day that goes by without a power failure and noise pollution due to the electric generators used as alternative sources of power to supply the many households.

Boarding a Lagos Molue Bus

Boarding a Train in Lagos

A Metro Station in Spain

Having observed firsthand the good roads and an efficient transport system, constant electricity, adequate communication, a clean environment, and a health system that topped it off, I reasoned that Germany was the place for me and a place worth living in. But living in Germany lies in the power of snagging a woman who is a German national. Without marriage to a German lady is near impossible to reside in the Deutsch land legitimately.

EXPERIENCING CULTURE SHOCK

Each country or people have customs that are peculiar only to them, but to the foreigner, these day to day customs certainly seem different and strange. It is said that one man's meat is another man's poison. I must say what I was shocked to observe what is considered the normal way of life in Germany compared to what I was used to back home.

ATTACHMENT TO DOGS

I was surprised to see how closely attached the whites are to dogs as pets. Almost everyone has a dog. And the care, love and attention given to the dogs even surpass that given to some foreigners or even family members. I saw all kinds of dogs and some well dressed in winter clothes. The owners of these dogs beam with happiness when they realize you like their dogs. They would tell you the history of the dog even to the second generation. I later learnt that most emergency ambulances that careen through the streets with their sirens blowing is usually an emergency involving a wounded dog needing to get to the veterinary clinic.

I was also taken aback with learning that friends and neighbors would make condolence calls to dog owners bereaved over a dog or pet dying. This was a sharp contrast to my country where the majority of people care little to nothing for dogs and pets. It did not end there! Just when I thought I had seen it all, I was in for an even bigger shock. In Germany, I witnessed dogs and pets going to church to partake in a religious ceremony which has been earmarked and reserved in the church calendar exclusively for the pets to receive benediction from the priest.

PUBLIC ROMANCE

I was shocked to see people kissing and expressing their affections to each other openly on the sidewalk, road, train, bus and public places without any shame or reservation especially among the young people who would be glued to each other kissing and caressing for what seemed like hours. Back in Nigeria this was not the practice, even in the cities. Things like that were done in private.

THE STRANGE DIETS

The sandwiches, salads and other kinds of foods were very strange to me. There was rouladen, and wienershnitzel (a type of pounded and breaded pork) and Spaetzle, (noodles served with gravy). The foods were indeed different and the various soups I had grown up with and fufu, the native delicacy I was used to was nowhere to be found. While German food is considered to be some of the best, it was a time of great deprivation for me. As my good friend would say, "I am a fufu fool." To which I say, "Give me fufu or give me death!"

UNFOLDING REALITIES

Life abroad is like a secret cult: you never know what is inside until you are initiated. Nobody tells you the downside to living abroad; they only speak of the rosy, beautiful, fanciful and appealing details of the other side of the coin. They dangle their sugar-coated lies about life abroad before their countrymen intending to make the same leap from home to the unknown. Even if one is told the reality, he may not believe the ugly details as normally we need to experience things firsthand in order to be convinced.

After two days in Oti's house, I was asked to leave. When I was in Nigeria preparing for this trip, my thought was that once I entered Europe with a visa, I would be staying and would renew the visa repeatedly. My cousin did not come to stay. He introduced me to Oti and left. Oti asked me on the first day if I came to stay or whether I would be going back soon. I told him of my intent to stay and his response was that I must declare myself a refugee, and if I claimed to come from any country in Africa where a war is presently brewing, this would fortify my case. Due to civil unrest, a native from Liberia or Cote d'Ivoire had the in to being declared a refugee. But that seemed strange and it literally was a shock to me. I told him I came here to work and not as a refugee. He laughed and said, "This is Germany and if you really wish to stay, you must become

a refugee first and then find a woman who will marry you
as this will give you permanent resident status."

My cousin's friend had passed through the system and
knew it well. When weighing the options facing me with
either becoming a refugee or having a woman marry me
to make my stay legal were very bitter pills to swallow. My
thoughts first went to the refugee camps I experienced as
a child during the Biafra war. It's not an experience that I
particularly wanted to repeat twice in a lifetime.

I also remembered the stories about Hitler and the Nazi
concentration camps. Since this was Germany, how did
I know whether those terrible war camps still existed or
whether they had been done away with? Also I have always
held marriage in high esteem and have always wished to
marry a woman I love and who loves me also. Marriage
of this kind would allow us to make a happy home and a
family. I never wanted to marry a woman based on what
she could offer me in terms of immigration status simply
to have a marriage of convenience. I therefore resolved that
if it's going to be, it's up to me and my God.

Since I was not compelled by anybody to embark on this
journey, I would rather face squarely whatever challenge
that came my way with faith in my God as He had proven
himself over and over to the Israelites and to those who
humbly call upon him. With His help, I would scale
through the hurdles. Seeing that there was no way the
asylum cup could pass over me except I drink it, I settled
for that. I truly felt that the unfolding realities were far
from what I expected or the impression of Europe I had
in my mind before leaving home. I had the impression

that Europe was a place full of jobs and business; a place you could enter and start work and start making money immediately. The reality at hand was far from that of the many Nigerian compatriots who came home with success stories touting that they could make it big in a relatively short interval of time, usually 3-6 months. They would send money and cars home to Nigeria, build houses and accomplish things they were not capable to achieve before leaving home. Where are the money-bearing trees people pluck while abroad I asked myself? Behind every sudden wealth there is a crime.

SEEKING ASYLUM

I was given the direction to a police station and I went and handed myself over to them. I was shivering from the cold as I entered their office. I guessed from their gesturing they were asking me what I wanted. I told them I was newly arrived and had no place to stay. They said "ausweis bitte" which means "document please?" I told them I had no document and that started a barrage of questions like where are you from, how did you come here, who brought you here, do you speak Dutch and so on, and I felt I needed a gargantuan mouth or the seven heads of a talking hydra to answer all these questions thrown to me at the same time.

I was thoroughly searched and my clothes and shoes were removed. I was taken inside a room which had a bed and a toilet, a veritable cell. The door had a pigeon hole and I was a caged bird. From time to time someone would come and peep through the pigeon hole to check on me. I was served coffee which I detest, but it was like ambrosia to me as my chilled body welcomed its warmth in my veins. They later brought a paper stating that I was been detained as an illegal immigrant without any document for my identification and stated that I had the right to request a lawyer. I was later interrogated by a lady lawyer who seemed to be polite and friendly however I was very careful not to let out information that would be detrimental to my plight knowing that the politeness may have been a subtle way to draw me out from my shell.

After the interview I was discharged and given a fare ticket for transport and a covering note from the police to allow me passage to the refugee camp located far away. I arrived at the camp late after much difficulty in locating the place as I disembarked at the wrong bus stop before the camp due to my language barrier. I had to trek a long distance in the rain and cold and arrived at the camp almost frozen by the winter cold.

The security guard turned me away stating that it was too late to admit anybody since there was no sleeping space available and they have already served dinner to the inmates. But I insisted and let him know that I did not know anyone nor did I have anywhere else to go from here. He was touched and let me inside to sleep in the dining hall with a blanket he provided for me. I have never been exposed to or felt cold like that in my life before. I have been bitten by the African sun, I have been scorched by my region's tropical weather, and now I have been chilled and frozen by the European cold and Germany's winter. With climate on opposite ends of the spectrum, my experience would be that my body and soul would emerge weather proof.

The camp was located on an anchored ship and served as a transitory dormitory for circumstantial refugees like myself. The asylum process was like being in the military. You had no place to call your own; you could be moved and transferred to a new location at any time. After few days on the ship, I was taken to the real refugee camp at Oldenburg.

That was where the real asylum journey started. This was where you were interrogated thoroughly and you had to state why you left your homeland to come to Germany. Your fate to remain for a short while or for a long duration in Germany would be decided from there. On arrival to Oldenburg, I was surprised to see people from all parts of the world as refugees in that camp: Russians, Polish, Romanians, Ecuadorians, and Peruvians—so very many cultures were represented there.

Oldenburg to me was like a vast plantation of humanity. To those who think that poverty, suffering and crisis are peculiar to one race and that Africa is the weeping child, from my experience at Oldenberg, your perspective changes radically and you are proved contrary. These inherent problems are like a cancer virus which has infected our world and a plague which humanity irrespective of color and race must wrestle with.

My stay in the refugee camp was like going back to the boarding house of my college days. There was a stipulated time for everything: eating, labor, games and sleep. One could not go outside without obtaining authorized permission from the house master. We interacted and made friends among the people of various nations. We ate from one pot—Black and white, Christians and Muslims under one roof. I saw humanity as one, one world, one God, one destiny. I could see that man is humble when he is in difficulty.

Each inmate looked forward to the interview day; it's like a D-day liberation to everyone in the camp awaiting their fate. Your mind could not be at rest until you have gone through the interview. You might have taken days and weeks to prepare and rehearse your story for the interview. It used to be a frenzied moment beyond that of preparing for the final year college certificate or final year university degree thesis and defense. It's a day you tell the story of your life in front of a video camera. It is also a day you must present convincing reasons and evidences why you left your homeland and must prove beyond reasonable doubt that you deserve a refuge in Deutschland.

In journalism it is said that good news is that which is bad. For example, dog bites man is not newsworthy, but man bites dog is news as it is out of the ordinary. Likewise all stories meant for refugee status hearings must bear that journalistic essence. You did not come for a picnic, and the interviewers don't have the ears for romantic stories. They want to hear about hardships, disasters, tragedy, catastrophe, genocide, war, hailstorms, and strange and life threatening dangers in your life.

No matter how phony and fabricated the story might be, if it was cooked to be like a palatable dish, it would be eaten. However pathetic and acceptable your story might be, your status must be reviewed after a time. While in the refugee camp, I became very popular among my colleagues for composing and developing stories for others. They would always refer newcomers to me as I would listen to their accounts and develop a story for them to present. In return, I never lacked beer and although beer was not allowed in the camp, it was always smuggled inside. My other form of payment for my journalistic flair was in bus tickets which were purchased for me whenever I had to go to the city.

There were some funny experiences during my stay in the asylum camp. It is usually said that fun things are even more fun when shared with others. The first time I went for a medical checkup after arriving the Oldenburg camp, the doctor asked me to lie on the bed facing up. He touched my tummy and said, "Baby, baby, exercise, exercise." I was somewhat perplexed by his comment. I guessed that as my tummy was big, he may have seen double and may have mistaken me as carrying a baby. And I reasoned that since this is a new world to me, it could be that men perhaps get pregnant in this part of the world.

To avoid any future incident of possibly being rushed to the operating theatre for a caesarian section, I responded by telling the doctor, "beer, beer," and he further responded, "exercise, exercise" and smiled. Actually when I arrived in Germany initially I had a pot belly which was a result of overindulging in beer in Nigeria in those happy days.

Going through the asylum process was not easy. After spending about three months at the refugee camp in Oldenburg, I was transferred to a village called Eggermulein at the outskirts of Beersenbruck. I would never forget my stay in Eggermuhlein where I shared a fine flat to with two other colleagues.

The village was a very fine and beautiful environment with new buildings, beautiful premises, flowers and landscaping. There were fields and recreation parks. I wondered how that could be a village compared to my native village. What is considered as a village in Germany and in Europe was like a GRA (government reserved area) in Nigeria. The GRAs in Nigeria are housing developments where the big wigs of society such as the politicians, high class entrepreneurs, and lumber magnates and the affluent live. It had a mark of class distinction. I wished I could transform my Ogele village to be like Eggermuhlein where all essential amenities for living seemed to be in place. While my flat mates considered the village remote and boring and they preferred to stay with their brothers and friends in the city, I remained in the village and socialized with the locals.

The villagers were friendly and nice to me. I had many friends in Eggermuhlein, both old and young. Among them were Dr. Karl Alberzt and his family, a medical practitioner who became friendly to me as I was the first black patient that came to his clinic. Another noteworthy couple of friends were Rakim Hiltz, the young man who had no other agenda for us except discotheques and music concerts around the city and Udo and Klaus, who would drive long distances to come and have Bible studies with me.

Acceptance into a society as an asylum seeker or immigrant is not that easy and I lived the experience. According to an Amnesty International report, "As the number of people seeking protection has increased, so too has the reluctance of states to provide that protection". After approximately one year in Germany, my attempt to reside in that country failed, and I was asked to leave the country. Despite the Governments tough policies on immigrants, from my own experience, individually the Germans are very warm, friendly and welcoming to foreigners and immigrants in their midst.

THE DILEMMA OF LIVING
IN SPAIN

"When the going gets tough, the tough gets going." Joseph P. Kennedy (1888-1969), Father of U.S. President John F. Kennedy. www.wikipedia.org. My coming to Spain was by chance because initially it was not in my plan. I decided to come to Spain instead of going back home because Germany did not grant me a residence permit.

For a black immigrant to live in Spain is akin to being a bull in a bull fight which the matador seeks to gore the very life out of you while you dodge his moves. Like the bull, you receive so many hard blows, but rather than blows of the matador's epee, they are blows of discrimination and racism. The choice to survive is yours if you are able to endure the hard blows and knocks.

The life of an immigrant is faced with severe hardships and uncertainties. And it's hard to find a stable and permanent refuge outside of home. After my asylum status crumbled in Germany, Spain became my new destination. Before coming to Spain, I was at a crossroads. I thought about going back to my country and starting all over again instead of wasting away the time of my life in Europe without engaging in something meaningful. I considered my abandoned university education, my thriving business and the client-list I had built after years of hard work and diligence. I thought of my family, friends, home, the long separation, my abandoned projects and my marriage that would be delayed because of leaving home. Despair could have entered my life at this point as the vision goal and the present life did not match up.

The moment I stepped out, others stepped in to occupy my space. How would I regain the positions and time and resources lost for coming to seek a better life abroad which seems to now be a mirage? So many thoughts ran through my mind. I thought about the future, and the virtues of patience, determination, faith and perseverance. I remembered that the future is greater than the past, and that winners don't quit and quitters never win. Also that tough times never last but tough people do.

Above all, I remembered my Bible which said that to him that believes, everything is possible. And that the earth and all that dwell in it belong to God. Armed with all these up-lifting thoughts from myself, from other men and from God, I encouraged myself to move on to Spain as obtaining a green card was easier in Spain than Germany. This weary pilgrim decided to forge onward instead of going back home. "If your mind jumps over the hurdle your body can't say no". Benson Idahosa (1938-1998) www.wikipedia.org

After two years in Spain I obtained my permanent residency and work permit. Nevertheless, it did not come on platter of gold as it was not easy to get a company that act as guarantor to show the government that you can sustain yourself should they grant you a residence permit. Until you obtain a residence permit (green card), you could not say you have arrived in Europe. Life in Europe is a regulated system. Until you are admitted into the system, you cannot do anything meaningful. Everything hinges on documentation and I have been residing and working in Spain since then.

Though the Spanish immigration law may seem to be more favorable and easier towards immigrants in Spain compared to Germany and other European states, the Spanish are individually discriminatory to foreigners, especially to the black Africans in particular. They isolate and make you feel unwelcome. That is a sharp contrast compared to the elaborate greetings and hospitality the Nigerians offer to foreigners in their midst. The Spanish are fearful and apprehensive at the invasion of foreigners to their country. They exhibit this attitude at work, on the trains and in public places. It's worse when you don't understand the language. A Spanish colleague at work once told me, "We don't like foreigners; we only pretend to like them."

I have been a victim of their discrimination several times. One occasion was when I worked at two jobs. One job would end and I would go to another. The second job required a corporate look so at the end of my day on the first job, I changed and put on my suit and tie. I quite like dressing fashionably for no particular occasion as it is my nature. That day my boss noticed me and asked me if I was travelling. I replied that I was going to work. That seemed like a big surprise to him, and he immediately retorted, 'como asii en este pais'. Meaning, like this in this country? A day later, I was fired for no justifiable reason.

The reason without any doubt was that as a black African, I was not supposed to do a corporate job or appear elegant. "If somebody hates you there is something in you he covets", (unknown). The job I was fired from required spoken English as a priority and I had an edge over my Spanish colleagues on that.

After that incident I devised a strategy. From that point on I always looked for employment in companies that requires bilingual personnel. With the advantage of knowing the English language, I exploit their lack of knowledge of English to my own advantage. In that case they would not look down on you much. Rather, they have to look up to you for assistance when English needs to be spoken and it has worked well for me.

My wife also has experienced this bullish attitude. When she was pregnant with our daughter Anabel, she was running errands and soon she needed to urinate so badly that she walked into a bar and requested to use the toilet. The man vehemently refused her the use of the restroom. She felt so bewildered and hurt as she thought that her pregnant condition would soften the man towards permitting her to use the toilet. However, that's a predicament she has to bear as a black immigrant in Spain.

Experience has thought me that living as an immigrant in Spain and Europe generally is not a bed of roses. You face severe employment restrictions, or underemployment, discrimination and ridicule. Many immigrants leave their home countries to look for a better life in other countries not from choice, or reasons of personal convenience but out of absolute necessity. For that reason many endure untold hardships. "Be it ever so humble, there's no place like home", John Howard Payne, (1791-1852/ New York City, New York). www.poemhunter.com

MISCONCEPTIONS, AND THE MYTH
OF THE WHITE RACE

The perceived superiority and inferiority complex between the white and black races was one of the reasons for leaving my homeland. I had read much, but in a predominantly black society, I needed to find out things for myself. It is said that experience is the best teacher. Having been privileged to taste both worlds I feel that I can honestly make the following remarks:

To the Europeans the African or black man is considered as savage and servile. He is seen as inferior to his white counterpart. But in my own view and observation, this is a misnomer and a misconception. The white man is by no means superior to his black counterpart if put on the same playing field. This has been proven in so many facets of life. For example, in politics, we have had likes of Nelson Mandela; in sports we have Mike Tyson, Serena Williams and Pele who have made great strides for the black athlete; in literature, Wole Soyinka and Chinua Achebe to name a few have penned great works; in music, Bob Marley and Michael Jackson have created harmonious melodies and arrangements; and in science, the Philip Egweani and the Chike Obi are noteworthy contributors to the field, to mention but a few.

The African's virtue of a good spirit of hospitality to strangers was initially misconstrued as weakness and was cashed in on by the scheming subtle Europeans who subtly sought to invade the black man's land to plunder and exploit his human and mineral resources to his own benefit.

The Africans were blind and ignorant of the western imperialism device from the beginning and left their doors wide open to let them in. The 19th century colonization of Africa through white missionaries and monopoly mercantile companies was an extension of the White's exploitation of the African continent. Slave trade, colonialism, neo-colonialism and the present day globalization were all exploitative mechanisms devised by the Westerners to suck the milk out of the African breast of plenty.

According to Emeka Ojukwu, the late Biafra head of state, on Ahiara Declaration (1969) "It suited them to transport and transplant millions of the flowers of our manhood for the purpose of exploring the Americas and western Indies. When it became no longer profitable to them to continue with depopulation and uncontrolled spoliation of Negro Africa, their need of the moment became to exploit the natural resources of the continent."

They install and support puppet rulers as presidents to create the impression of political independence, while retaining the control of the economy behind the scene. In spite of their orchestrated open pronouncement to the contrary, the white peoples of the world especially the

Europeans are still far from accepting that what is good for them can also be good for black Africans.

The days they will concede to this recognition, those days will the dream of one world be realized. Because the black man is considered inferior and servile to the white man, I could not wear my suit to work, and my wife could not be allowed to answer the call of nature. Whether a corporate businessman or a janitor, I am a man who enjoys fashion and looking good so it is not unusual to see me sporting a suit. Also, the black man must accept all dehumanizing conditions, job restrictions, and underemployment while living in Spain.

On the opposite side of the coin, in Africa and in Nigeria, even the least qualified white man working at a company is chauffeur driven and occupies a strategic job position. That is the road our ancestors went. That is the road we met up with. That is the road we have been on. And this is the road we cannot continue following.

I call on Africans and fellow blacks to awaken from slumber and face the realities of your situation. Nobody will do it for you better than you ought to. We have all it takes to greatness but we have been ignorant and blind about using our own resources and talents to recreate our own world. We Africans, we have to learn how to live our lives without scripts; not to stand as onlookers and watch others crack our kernels for us. We should not allow our limitations to limit us. Even when we know there are many limitations, in the midst of them are equally huge opportunities which have gone unnoticed. We can make it if we really want to.

ANSWERS TO WEIGHTY QUESTIONS

"Nobody can go back and start a new beginning, but anyone can start today and make a new ending." Maria Robinson, www.thinkexist.com. Regardless of the success or failures of the past we should not remain passive, rather we should always re-ignite the courage to continue from where we failed or stopped.

As mentioned earlier in the introduction, the road we travelled is the story of an African child who walked two different paths with so many hardships, struggles, difficulties and challenges. For me as an individual, the battle to overcome imposing hardships, poverty and obstacles helped me to become the person that I am by attaining awareness through education and knowing more about the outside world.

I still pose the question as to why nature's resources are not evenly distributed. Or how do some people become successful and wealthier than others? Why do some nations appear happier and more contented than others? And why should one leave his home land to look for a life in another country?

And as Solomon, I can sit and ponder all the whys of why something is as it is, or is not as it should be. My conclusions are that the world is a vast plantation. Life is a journey and the road to attain success and happiness is not easy. For me, it's been a rocky road in search of success and happiness. Likewise the same pursuit applies to my tribe, nation, race and humanity at large.

I have weathered through some of the storms and obstacles that were on my road right from birth. I never had an affluent parental background. But through hard work, self-determination, courage and discipline I made up for my lack. The road we travelled is the story of the life journey of an old friend of mine, that transcends to the experience of others, and humanity at large. And that friend is me.

We survived a gruesome bloodbath in a civil war, lack of the basic amenities of life due to poverty and a great lack of education. It was living by the sweat of your brow and self-determination. But even within the toll of living the everyday life, the African family tie to a fraternity has always been a stronghold second to none.

Today, looking back to the beginning, there have been some remarkable changes, improvements, and failures on the road we travelled. In life, you win some, and you lose some. Forty five years ago our source of light used to be the palm oil lamp. Today we switch on lights and electricity illuminates our living quarters. Ponds have been replaced by tap water embedded in our walls and compounds. Letters and communication that used to take months are now communication modes that are almost immediate with the telephone and internet connections. The mud and thatched roof houses have been replaced with block and corrugated zinc houses.

On the other hand, the primary and secondary schools we attended are in a sorry state of decay today as they have been neglected by the government. The rail system of transport we enjoyed during my college days has collapsed and been abandoned. My country Nigeria has not achieved the desired unity and peace it fought for. Forty two years after the civil war, the unity of the country is today being threatened by those who never wanted Nigeria to exist as one great nation.

I leapt into the white man's world and moved to Europe. I witnessed firsthand the realities of the black man living in Europe with its winter deep freeze, and its culture shock foreign to me. I witnessed the difference between the Germans and the Spaniards in their attitude to foreigners like me. I met Anita, a wonderful Canadian lady who shattered a lot of my beliefs about the white race. We share such a caring, genuine friendship second to none.

Beyond the shores of Nigeria, racism and discrimination still reign in the mind of people. The black man is still considered inferior by his white counterpart. Standing at a crossroad in my journey, conflicts have been established in my heart about leaving home weighed against my disappointments at learning that Europe was not the paradise and Promised Land I thought it would be. And the conceived superiority of whites over blacks in fact was a misconception of reality. In spite of the West's orchestrated aid to Africa, they still wish Africa would remain a child, dependent on foreign aid and hand-outs.

Man is inferior to his fellow man only if he chooses to be. The world will know no peace until the day man stops trying to dominate and rule over his fellow man. The passage of so many years away from home will never wipe off the memories of my native land. Moreover, in my own view, racism and discrimination is not peculiar to the Spanish, Europeans, or whites. No, it is a cancer which has eaten deep into the entire human race. Its starts with the family and spans to the tribe, nation and race.

Among children of one parent, there is a favorite child. Favoritism is a bed fellow to racism. From family and parental favoritism it germinates to tribal discrimination, nationalism, and then matures to racism. Therefore it's a human factor, and mankind's problem, and is beyond man's solution. Because from the beginning man was designed to lean on a supernatural being to lead him.

Until mankind realizes his origin and subscribes to his maker, then will his mind be absolved from all discrimination and hatred on the road he or she travels. Until then, our world will not know peace nor become the one world we are craving for. "The heart is deceitful above all things, and desperately wicked: Who can know it? Holy Bible Jeremiah 17:9 King James Version (KJV). I believe that it is only Omnipotent, Omnipresent being, God the Father that can tame the heart of man from all wickedness, hatred and racism and bring peace in the world, which I see as a vast plantation.

THE VAST PLANTATION

In the beginning of creation were you
So large you are,
Mankind is the crop found in you
Planted of different species by the planter
In different locations and time
Various crops have spring forth from you
Some are white, and some are black
Some are yellow, and some are red

Some though planted
Never grew up to see the day light
Many have stunted growth
Some planted in fertile lands
Produced poor yields
Some found in not quite fertile lands
Produced better yields
The planter sends reapers
To harvest everyday

There is no time crops are lacked in the field
Some are harvested when unripe,
Others ripe, but ignored
Some with greenish leaves
Are at the prime of life
Others have faded leaves
Which soon will be shaded off?
Planting and harvesting will continue in you
Until the planter decides to plant no more.

CONCLUSION

L ooking back to the past, the road we traveled was littered with so many obstacles and challenges that needed to be surpassed. But with determination, hard work, education, confidence and faith in God, most of those obstacles and challenges have been conquered, while some still remain. However, whatever the situation may be, our resolve should be to recreate our own world and leave the world better than we met it.

The diversified experiences in my life, exposure, knowledge and education currently obtained have afforded me opportunities that would have been passed by. I foresee a better life, and a brighter future, where I will earn more and will reward my family with a better life, vacations at choice places, and I hope to be in a place where I can award scholarships to children from poor homes in my community.

I have always attached a great importance to education and have wished to learn and excel in life. Though my wife and family have been very supportive of my education, I have seen how hard it is to work and go to school or for one to fend for him in school. Therefore I will always encourage my children, and young ones to always strive and complete their education on time before life's responsibilities creep in.

My counsel for my tribe, nation, Africa and the black race is that you cannot go back to relive the past, but you can start today to build a better tomorrow and make a new ending. You don't wait until everything is right, because it will never be that perfect. There will always be challenges, barriers, and less than perfect conditions. So you must stand and face your challenges until you succeed. You can make it if you really want. Start cracking your kernels today and don't wait for another person to crack them for you.

To the Spanish, my host country, I love you; you are my bird in the hand that is worth more than ten in the bush. We are inextricably involved with each other. I am a resident, but my daughter is a native as she was born in Spain. Though living in Spain has not been easy, it has been very beneficial and rewarding for me.

To the rest of the world and humanity, consider the road mankind has traveled, it may not have been smooth and jolly for the entire human race as we may not have been fair and nice to each other. But we can start today to mend fences, and to heal our world. Where hatred and discrimination have dominated, let love and tolerance take possession.

Let us sing a new love song for the world, and heal our world of the wounds we have caused it, and make it a better place for the human race to live in. And let humanity remember that we are children of one father. Therefore, let one love reign and keep us together as one.

Life is a journey, the world is a vast plantation, and we are all pilgrims on a journey, via the road we travel presently and on the roads we came.

REFERENCES

1. Joel Osteen,(Pastor Lakewood Church, Texas U.S.A) www.twitter.com   IX
2. (Author Unknown)   X
3. Richard Le Gallienne, www.virual.fundamentals.smugmug   X
4. Eyamide Coker – African Proverbs,Parables and Wie Sayings (2011,Paperback)   3
5. Myles Munroe, President and Founder of the Bahamas Faith Ministries International (BFMI)   5
6. African Proverbs in African Literature, www.proverbsafricanliterature.wordpress.com   12
7. Innocent Nkhonyo – The Wisdom of Africa, www.poemhunter.com   14
8. Horatius Bonar (1808 – 1889)   19
9. (African `Proverbs) – www. Ocean-anaedo.org   20
10. Hebrews 12:6 King James Bible (Cambridge Ed.)   21
11. Wikipedia Reference   27
12. Jeanne Ukwendu, African Proverbs on Pregnancy and Birth, www.bellaonline.com   30
13. Deciderius Erasmus (28 October 1466 – 12 July 1536) – www.wikipedia.org   34
14. Henry Wadsworth Longfellow, www.quoteworld. org   34
15. (Author Unknown), www.searchquotes.com   37

16. Malcolm X (19 May 1925 – 21 February 1965), www.wikipedia.org   38
17. (African Proverbs)   45
18. Proverbs 22: 6 Holy Bible King James Version (KJV)   59
19. Mark Twain quotes. (American Humorist, Writer and Lecturer. 1835-1910), www.thinkexist .com   61
20. Dr. Myles Muroe (The Bahamas Faith Ministries International BFMI). www.wikipedia.org   63
21. Proverbs 18:22 Holy Bible King James Version (KJV)   74
22. Cyprian   Ekwensi   –   African   Night Entertainment   74
23. African Proverbs, www.ezinnearticles.com   77
24. Ruby K. Payne, PhD, www.gazettextra.com   81
25. T. Harv Eker. Secrets of the Millionaire Mind (Harper Business an Imprint of Harper Collins Publishers). www.harpercollins.com   82
26. Mathew 7: 7 Holy Bible King James Version (KJV)   83
27. Joseph P. Kennedy (1888-1969), Father of U.S. President John F. Kennedy. www.wikipedia.org   101
28. Benson   Idahosa   (1938-1998)   www.wikipedia. org   102
29. John Howard Payne, (1791-1852/ New York City, New York). www.poemhunter.com   104
30. Emeka Ojukwu THE AHIARA DECLARATION (The Principles of the Biafran Revolution)   106
31. Maria Robinson, www.thinkexist.com.   108
32. Jeremiah 17:9 Holy Bible King James Version (KJV)   111